C0-AWA-143

Christian Voices

JOURNEYS THROUGH FAITH AND POLITICS IN CONTEMPORARY AMERICAN PROTESTANTISM

Charlene Floyd

RECEIVED

FEB 14 2008

MINNESOTA STATE UNIVERSITY
MANKATO, MN 56002-8419

PRAEGER

Westport, Connecticut
London

BR
515
.F46
2007

Library of Congress Cataloging-in-Publication Data

Floyd, Charlene, 1962–
   Christian voices : journeys through faith and politics in contemporary American
Protestantism / Charlene Floyd.
   p. cm.
   Includes bibliographical references and index.
   ISBN 978-0-275-99002-2 (alk. paper)
   1. Protestantism—United States. 2. Protestant churches—United States—Doctrines. 3.
Christianity and politics—United States. I. Title.
   BR515.F46 2007
   261.70973—dc22   2007010724

British Library Cataloguing in Publication Data is available.

Copyright © 2007 by Charlene Floyd

All rights reserved. No portion of this book may be
reproduced, by any process or technique, without the
express written consent of the publisher.

Library of Congress Catalog Card Number: 2007010724
ISBN-13: 978-0-275-99002-2
ISBN-10: 0-275-99002-8

First published in 2007

Praeger Publishers, 88 Post Road West, Westport, CT 06881
An imprint of Greenwood Publishing Group, Inc.
www.praeger.com

Printed in the United States of America

The paper used in this book complies with the
Permanent Paper Standard issued by the National
Information Standards Organization (Z39.48–1984).

10 9 8 7 6 5 4 3 2 1

6516055

For Jessie, Harry, and K—this book belongs to you

For my father who taught me what matters

Contents

Acknowledgments

This is a book of amazing stories, journeys of faith that moved and surprised the teller as much as the listener. These are stories of personal transformation, of connections to the Savior, of miracles of divine thinking and divine living. Few people realized they even had a story until they began to tell it. But once they started, the hours passed and revelation poured forth.

It is the generosity of spirit and time of many good people that made this project possible: friends at St. Francis United Methodist Church: Sandy DeVoid, Ben DeVoid, Alex and Hannah DeVoid, Kevin Ward, Jim Carter, Dan Purcell, Penny Purcell, and Debra Pressley; friends at Concord Presbyterian Church: Ginny Teitt, Jim Teitt, Tony Eyerman, Stephanye Harris, and Pam Stockdale; friends at Park Slope United Methodist Church: Dorothy Benz, Herb Miller, Judy Fram, Carol Scott, and Kathy Dickinson; friends at Second Baptist Church: Beverly Gambrell, Jack Little, Skip McBride, Lisa Milne, Fred Williams, Kellye Williams, Dr. Ed Young, and Archie Dunham; and friends at home: Karen Behm, Ron Bennett, Joy and Roger Floyd, Melinda Floyd, Ken Guest, Rusty Hesse, Elizabeth Jensen, bj Karpen, Jo and Bob Karpen, Julia Reidhead, Jim Ring, Lester Ruiz, Sarah Scheck, Susan Scheck, and Jane Williams. My heartfelt thanks to all of you.

Finally, to my family, Jessie, Harry, and K: we all agree this book has enough words and besides you, my dearest friends, are each in your own way a blessing in my life too big for words. Muchisimas gracias.

All scripture quotations are from the New Revised Standard Version.

1

Introduction

*H*ow does a person of faith determine his priorities? How does she perceive the world around her and ultimately make political decisions?

Religious undercurrents continue to galvanize political events in the United States as key political leaders make explicit their religious commitments and key religious leaders make explicit their political commitments. This phenomenon is accompanied by a sense of empowerment, even entitlement, on the part of some people of faith and, at the same time, by a deep-rooted misunderstanding and mistrust among and within religious communities throughout the country. It is in this tumultuous context that this book gives voice to a variety of Protestant Christians with an eye toward understanding how people who share the same scriptures, hymns, prayers, and sometimes even creeds arrive at and embrace radically different political perspectives. For example, why do evangelical Christians believe they have a biblical mandate to oppose abortion, stem cell research, and gay marriage? Or, on the other hand, why do progressive Christians believe they are called to be "the voice of the voiceless": to advocate for the poor, the excluded, and those who suffer the effects of an aggressive U.S. foreign policy?

The interplay of religion and politics is a hot topic, both in academia and among the general public. Not surprisingly, books about this topic are no longer a rarity.[1] What distinguishes *Christian Voices* from many of these books is not the subject matter, but the way in which this material is addressed: what might be referred to as the book's soul. Richly detailed personal histories and congregational stories comprise the body of the work. Seasoned believers rather than seasoned academics, theologians, politicians, or activists are given voice. Those doing the talking are people whose names the reader probably will not recognize. And yet, the thoughts about presidents and protest marches, prayers and piano lessons, Bible studies and Christmas pageants, and marathons and mission trips will not seem strange. The reasons for celebrating: happy holidays, loving relationships, church building, hymn singing, and children growing; and the causes of despair: the loss of a child, of a sibling, or of meaningful employment; the reality of poverty, exclusion, and religious divisions will be familiar, at times painfully so. Reading these profiles one might begin to answer those basic questions: "How can *they* call themselves Christian?" and "How could *they* possibly have voted for *him*?"

SLIPPING THROUGH THE HEDGE

When questioned on the subject, people often assert that the Constitution of the United States requires the separation of church and state, directing their examiner to the First Amendment. Though the First Amendment does address the issue of religion, it does not call for the separation of church and state. The amendment states, "Congress shall make no law respecting an establishment of religion, or prohibiting the free exercise thereof," commonly referred to as the Establishment Clause and the Free-Exercise Clause. The former forbids the government from aligning itself with or advocating on behalf of a particular religious tradition, and the latter protects the rights of individuals to engage in the religious practice of their choosing without interference from the government.

Both the Free-Exercise and the Establishment Clause are vague enough to have engendered considerable debate over the years,[2] though there is substantial evidence that the two men responsible for the inclusion of religious freedom in the Constitution, Thomas Jefferson and James Madison, favored a clearly delineated separation of church and state. For his part, Jefferson argued for "a wall of separation" between church and state, though the phrase appears nowhere in the Constitution or the Bill of Rights. Whether the issue is prayer in school, the display of a community crèche at Christmas, support of religious educational institutions, or the selection of a science curriculum, feelings run deep and no answer is simple. What is clear is that the wall, if it ever did exist, might be better described today as a hedge where those who are willing to push a little can usually find a way through.

Adopting the Jeffersonian interpretation, Andrew Kohut et al. observe, "The First Amendment of the U.S. Constitution erected a high wall between church and state, but no such barrier exists between religion and politics. Religion is, and always has been, woven into the fabric of American political life."[3] The distinction between church and state/religion and politics is particularly useful in the context of *Christian Voices,* which focuses not on religious or political institutions, but on individual Christians.

One of the most celebrated recent examples of the way in which religion and politics (and for that matter church and state) have become tangled together is the case of All Saints Episcopal Church in Pasadena, California. Based upon its analysis of a single sermon by a guest preacher, delivered two days before the 2004 presidential election, the Internal Revenue Service (IRS) began investigating this liberal Protestant church for possible violations of the 1954 law prohibiting churches (and all nonprofit organizations) from partisan political involvement. The sermon in question described an imaginary debate between the two presidential candidates, Republican George W. Bush and Democrat John Kerry, during which Jesus offered his own critique of the political positions of the presidential hopefuls. With a long history of progressive activism, dating back to its outspoken opposition to the internment of Japanese Americans during World War II, none of which evoked an IRS response, many at All Saints Episcopal Church wonder about the timing and the motivation of the government's action.

Though federal law prohibits the IRS from releasing information about current investigations (the All Saints investigation became public only after the church itself chose to speak about it), by all accounts the IRS has stepped up its scrutiny of nonprofit organizations, particularly religious organizations, following the tremendous increase in political activity during the 2004 presidential election. Though some argue the church's progressive politics have caused All Saints to be targeted unfairly, it is important to note that Jerry Falwell Ministries, a well-known conservative Christian organization, has also been investigated and forced to make changes, particularly in its fund-raising strategies.

This government scrutiny is one of very few issues around which the religious community in the United States is unified. At a press conference where he announced that All Saints would not comply with IRS requests for documents or personal testimonies, Rev. Ed Bacon, the church's rector, was joined by Christian, Jewish, and Islamic leaders. Richard Land, a noted conservative evangelical, also publicly questioned the motives of this IRS action.

The IRS is at the heart of a passionate struggle on the other side of the country, at East Waynesville Baptist Church in North Carolina, as well. Rev. Chan Chandler openly endorsed Republican incumbent George W. Bush from the pulpit and questioned the religious convictions of parishioners who did not accept this choice. Though Rev. Chandler stands by his remarks, which he maintains centered mainly on the issue of abortion, the church was split. Those unwilling to align themselves with their pastor's political positions found it necessary to leave. Ultimately, facing an IRS investigation, Rev. Chandler resigned and some of the former members returned. However, a number of Chandler's supporters left along with him, and the small Baptist church is struggling to rebuild its religious community.

The 2004 presidential election was a defining moment in the relationship of religion and politics within the United States. *Washington Post* staff writer Alan Cooperman agrees, but takes it one step further, "Religion was not just a defining issue in the campaign but a divisive one."[4] He notes that voters who claimed to attend church more than once a week tended to vote for George W. Bush over John Kerry by an almost 2:1 margin. Though it was not the case in all states,[5] same-sex marriage ballot initiatives often galvanized religious, conservative voters benefiting the Republican Party (GOP for Grand Old Party).

The 2006 midterm election prompted renewed efforts on the Right, and on the Left, to encourage Christians to become involved in the political arena. Though initially planning to stay on the sidelines, Focus on the Family founder James Dobson decided he could not accept the ramifications of a Republican defeat in the House and the Senate. He began a speaking tour urging thousands of voters around the country, with a particular focus on eight battleground states, to vote their values. A new organization, Red-Letter Christians, offered progressive Christians opportunities to get involved in the elections. The group was founded by the Washington-based Sojourners community, whose leader, Jim Wallis, is a key actor on the evangelical Left. Like some of its more conservative counterparts, most notably the Christian Coalition, Red-Letter Christians distributed thousands of voter guides; though it delicately avoided issues like abortion and same-sex marriage that might prove divisive.

For much of the twentieth century, at least until the height of the civil rights movement, the Left was the dominant religious voice influencing American politics. The Supreme Court's *Roe v. Wade* decision and the subsequent formation of Jerry Falwell's Moral Majority, coupled with the increasing secularization of the country's liberal elite, paved the way for a sea change in which conservative evangelical voices began to gain strength. After George W. Bush secured over three-quarters of the evangelical vote in the 2004 presidential race, many in that community expected to see progress on their family-values agenda. In 2006, some evangelicals expressed concerns that the GOP may have taken the religious community's support for granted.

In this volatile political climate, former Republican Senator John Danforth sounded a call for moderate Christians to step forward. In his book *Faith and Politics: How the "Moral Values" Debate Divides America and How to Move Forward Together,*[6] Danforth argues that it is time for the Republican Party to disengage itself from the Christian Right. Others, like Rev. Rick Warren, author of the best-selling *The Purpose-Driven Life,*[7] are encouraging evangelicals to expand their agenda to include issues such as the environment and poverty in addition to family values.

Clearly there are connections between religion and politics. And whether one looks to Jefferson, or to those who are profiled in the following pages, it is also clear that politicians should never be permitted to set the agenda for a people of faith. Strong faith commitments, more often than not, translate into political commitments. But faith must always lead and politics must always follow.

Will evangelicals continue to wield substantial political influence, and, if so, where will their priorities lie? Will the religious Left build an effective organization and galvanize support sufficient to become a political force with which to be reckoned? Will the voices calling for moderation succeed in finding middle ground? The answers to these questions remain to be seen; but one thing is certain, religion is on, and will remain on, the table. It may not always be the main course, but like the sweet potatoes at Thanksgiving, the meal would not be complete without it.

KEY THEMES

In the following pages faith stories unfold. For some there is clarity. The Bible is true. A Christian seeks obedience to the Word. No one should be excluded. Who we are is a gift from God. Heaven exists, and so does Hell. A Christian's first allegiance is to the cross. But as often as not, one person's clarity is the cause of another's confusion.

Some have passionately argued that there are many roads to the Kingdom: Protestants finding comfort in the Catholic rosary or inspiration in the Jewish Passover Haggadah. Others have committed themselves to sharing the Gospel, dedicating their lives to helping others accept Jesus as "The Way." There are those who connect to Jesus, down and dirty, knocking over tables in the temple and those who speak of ways Satan is alive and well in today's society.

Some come from long lines of churchgoers, happily reminiscing about lemonade on the church lawn or donning the homemade halo and angel wings in the annual Christmas pageant. They recall the casseroles and apple pies that filled the kitchen table during times of mourning and the sense of security a child finds in knowing where he or she belongs. Others found their way to Christianity much later in life under an open-air tent one summer morning, in a swimming pool during those last few laps, or at the office after a long and difficult meeting.

Regardless of when or where, each of these Christians has been transformed by his or her faith and has sought to be in community with others who share the same convictions and experiences. For some the singing moves them to tears, old hymns taking her back to her grandmother's lap, or to an infant daughter sleeping in his arms. Others treasure times of silence, being quiet together. Sermons that speak the truth and prod the spirit are important. And there are questions: about the ordination of women, the role of young people, the incessant push for more and more members. Parishioners wonder about mission work: the connection between building a house and saving a soul. Whose soul needs saving? And pastors wonder how to clarify their call, provide a prophetic voice, and still nurture wounded souls.

Prayer is vitally important to every one of these Christians. Some have seen prayer transform death into life, and others had only prayer to sustain them as they saw a life end in death. They cherish the time spent in quiet, alone with their God. Many yearn to make more space in their lives for this precious gift.

At first glance one might question what bearing any of these seemingly personal portraits have on the social and political lives of these 16 people. Their stories of faith are relevant because each of the individuals profiled in the following chapters participates, on some level, in the American political system. And, without exception, each of them unequivocally claims that his or her faith is the most important factor shaping his or her political decisions. Some have dedicated their lives to reforming church polity, while others have grown weary of the institutional battles. Some bristle when they hear politics discussed from the pulpit, and others relish the opportunity for a healthy political debate during Bible study. Some pray President George W. Bush will continue to do God's work, while others pray he will see the Light and change his course. But every Christian in this book prays willingly and regularly for the President of the United States of America.

THREE DENOMINATIONS: UNITED METHODIST, PRESBYTERIAN, AND SOUTHERN BAPTIST

In many ways the stories that are told in the pages that follow address concerns and beliefs that would resonate with not only a wide range of Protestants, but with Christians in general. Nonetheless, these are the tales of individual Christians who are intimately connected to particular religious communities. At times these individuals proudly embrace their denominational affiliation, drawing strength from the traditions and the teachings of those who have preceded them. But there are also moments when some of the faithful bridle under the institutional attempts to move their part of the Body of Christ in ways that seem to them nothing short of un-Christian. In order to make sense of the individual's relationship to his or her denominational context, a brief overview of the three groups under consideration is provided.

The United Methodist Church

The United Methodist Church (UMC) currently has well over 8 million members and 34,892 churches throughout the United States. It also has close to 2 million members and almost 7,000 churches outside of the United States. Although United Methodist membership is declining in the United States, church membership in Asia and Africa has seen a substantial increase.

The United Methodist Church was formed in 1968 as the result of a merger between The Methodist Church and the Evangelical United Brethren Church. Methodism began as a movement within the Church of England in the 1730s with Anglican priest John Wesley spearheading the effort. In 1784 the Methodists in the United States created the Methodist Episcopal Church and Methodism officially became a denomination. In the mid-1800s the church split over the issue of slavery, reuniting again in 1939 as The Methodist Church. However, the church remained largely segregated until the 1968 merger.

Methodism in the United States has a vibrant tradition of connectional-ism that was initially fostered by the circuit riders, preachers, and lay minis-ters who rode horseback throughout the late 1700s and early 1800s preaching and otherwise ministering to frontier communities. Methodists also became known for their part in dramatic revivals and tent meetings dur-ing the Second Great Awakening.

Born out of John Wesley's fervent desire to minister to coal miners and other workers in Great Britain during the Industrial Revolution, Methodism has a long tradition of active social involvement. Many, but not all, Method-ists worked to end slavery. Many U.S. churches were damaged during the course of the Civil War in what some observers refer to as the physical mani-festation of the spiritual wounds suffered by The Methodist Church, divided by the issue of slavery. Methodists also played a leadership role in the temper-ance movement that emerged in the late 1800s. In the early 1900s, a progressive social creed was adopted, and many in The Methodist Church urged negotiation and arbitration as an alternative to violent confrontation on the international front. A significant pacifist voice arose in The Methodist Church. This was considerably weakened after the U.S. military became involved in World War II.[8]

Today The United Methodist Church is grappling to adjust to the increasingly global nature of its constituency while at the same time address-ing social issues, such as homosexuality, which are of particular concern to its members in the United States. The UMC continues to play a significant social and political role in the United States. In the 109th Congress there were 11 United Methodist senators and 50 United Methodist representatives, and both the president, George W. Bush and the vice president, Richard Cheney, belong to the denomination.[9] A broad, nondoctrinal denomination, United Methodists span the theological and political spectrum between quite conservative and very liberal.

The Presbyterian Church (U.S.A.)

In 1517 Martin Luther, a German priest, called into question the author-ity of the Roman Catholic Church, sparking a movement now known as the Protestant Reformation. Two decades later, lawyer and theologian John Calvin further developed these ideas about the nature of God and God's rela-tionship to humankind. His ideas spread throughout much of Europe. The Presbyterian Church was born out of this Reformed, or Calvinist, theological movement.

Rev. Francis Makemie came to what is now the United States in 1683. Some 23 years later he assisted with the organization of the first American Presbytery in Philadelphia. Four decades after that, the College of New Jersey (now known as Princeton University) was founded by Presbyterian clergy. Rev. John Witherspoon, a Presbyterian minister, was the president of

Princeton University from 1768 to 1793 and the only clergyman to sign the Declaration of Independence.

Though the denomination is small, the Presbyterian Church (U.S.A.) has not quite 2,500,000 members in 11,000 churches in each of the 50 states and Puerto Rico; its political influence has been, and continues to be, significant. There have been ten Presbyterian presidents (twice the number of Methodists) in the course of U.S. history. Fifteen Presbyterian senators and 37 Presbyterian representatives served in the 109th U.S. Congress.[10]

Similar to the Methodists, the Presbyterians became a church divided in the years prior to the Civil War. Some permanently left the denomination. Those who remained continued to struggle with theological and social issues after the war ended. Though the issues were complex, most observers accept the characterization of the struggle as one between the Modernists, who believed it necessary to reinterpret Christianity in light of changes in the modern world, and the Fundamentalists, who maintained that an unchanging Bible is at the heart of the faith. In the mid-1970s the dispute crystallized around the issue of the ordination of women, which was eventually accepted in the Presbyterian Church. A block of conservative churches split from the Presbyterian Church in 1973, primarily over the issue of the ordination of women, which they opposed. They formed the Presbyterian Church in America. Ten years later, in 1983, the United Presbyterian Church USA and the Presbyterian Church US united to form the Presbyterian Church (U.S.A.), finally healing the North-South split in the church.

The ordination of homosexual people recently provoked a similar debate. In 2006, the General Assembly voted to allow a "local option" to presbyteries with regard to ordination, although the Book of Order, which prohibits the gay and lesbian ordination, still stands. It is unclear how the 2006 vote will affect church policy.

The Presbyterian Church has a historical commitment to taking the Christian message out into the world. In 1837 the General Assembly declared "the church by its very nature, is a missionary society." As such the Presbyterian Church is involved in projects to overcome poverty, to encourage local development, to provide emergency relief, and to encourage education initiatives. Recently the Presbyterian Church (U.S.A.) General Assembly made headlines worldwide when it recommended a divestment campaign focused on corporations operating in Israel. Some congregations within the denomination, fearing the church has lost its biblical focus, have begun exploring options, including the possibility of leaving the denomination.[11]

The Southern Baptist Convention

The Baptist presence in America dates from the time of Roger Williams, who established a Baptist Church in Providence, Rhode Island, in 1639. In 1814, motivated by a need for foreign mission work, a nationwide General

Convention was formed. Like the Methodists and the Presbyterians, the Baptists were also caught up in the struggles prior to the Civil War. Some Baptists in the South doubted the denomination's claims of neutrality on the issue of slavery and, after their misgivings proved to be correct, seceded from the Triennial Convention of Baptists, forming the Southern Baptist Convention. In 1995, the Southern Baptist denomination formally repudiated the racism that prompted its formation and apologized for its defense of slavery.

The largest of the three denominations, with over 16 million members and more than 42,000 churches, the Southern Baptist Convention is also in some ways the sparest when it comes to denominational structure. Since its founding in Augusta, Georgia, in 1845, the Southern Baptist Convention has met for only a few days each year. Messengers, as the delegates are known, elected by their churches, attend the Convention. Unlike the United Methodists and the Presbyterians, the Southern Baptist Convention is not involved with the ordination or licensing of ministers. The Southern Baptist Convention has no authority to ordain or defrock its clergy; this is an entirely "local church matter." Given that this and many other issues involving church polity are taken care of on the local level, some have questioned the need for a denominational body. However, one important function of the Southern Baptist Convention is the coordination of extensive mission efforts at home and abroad. Well over 10,000 Southern Baptist missionaries serve in over 150 nations in an effort to share the Gospel of Jesus Christ with the entire world.

Though there may be a very limited number of exceptions, the vast majority of Southern Baptist Churches adhere to basic biblical beliefs. In other words, they would concur with the statements adopted and reconfirmed by the 1925 and 1963 Southern Baptist Conventions affirming, "The Holy Bible was written by men divinely inspired and is the record of God's revelation of Himself to man...It has God for its author, salvation for its end, and truth, without any mixture of error, for its matter...."[12] In 1987, the Southern Baptist Peace Committee of the Southern Baptist Convention reinforced this position by recommending that Southern Baptist educational institutions engage only professional leadership whose actions reflect this position. Many viewed this step as a signal that the conservative voice within the Convention had gained an influential majority with agenda-setting power.

The Convention also states that although "women are equal in value to men," scriptural teaching precludes women's participation in the pastoral leadership of the church. Although this assertion caused considerable uproar outside the Southern Baptist community, the membership has accepted it with little difficulty. Similarly, in 1998, messengers adopted an addition to their Baptist Faith and Message statement declaring that wives should "submit graciously" to their husbands.[13] Again, those who were not members of the denomination were troubled. For those familiar with the church, this simply represented an "official statement" of a routine church teaching. Neither the Depression, the Second World War, the civil rights struggle, nor the Vietnam War elicited an addition to the Message. The family-values debate of the late 1990s, however, was thought to demand the clarification of the Baptist stand on gender roles.

There have been four Baptist presidents. The 109th Congress counted seven Baptist senators and 68 Baptist representatives, many of whom are Southern Baptist, among its numbers.[14]

OVERVIEW OF CONGREGATIONS

It is important to note at the outset that this work is comprised of less than 20 interviews. Though a wide variety of thoughts and ideas are expressed, the group consists of white, middle and upper class Protestants. Protestant churches are richly blessed with economic, ethnic, and racial diversity, pointing toward the need for further and broader studies of this type.

Each chapter recounts individual faith journeys told within the context of a particular religious community. Since the purpose of this project is to give voice to particular religious and political perspectives, each of those profiled has carefully reviewed and is satisfied with his or her portrayal. Extensive quotations derived from in-depth interviews allow the voices of those being profiled to be clearly heard and allows the reader to gain real insights from the lives of real people.

Chapter 2 focuses on St. Francis United Methodist Church in Charlotte, North Carolina. Under the direction of Pastor Ben DeVoid (who has since taken on the role of Senior Pastor at Dilworth United Methodist Church, also in Charlotte), St. Francis focused much of its energy on mission work: in Charlotte, in the nearby Appalachian Mountains, on the Gulf Coast, and outside the United States in Mexico and Jamaica. Sandy DeVoid, a trained Christian educator, oversaw the small but vital youth ministry at the church, which, as each of those interviewed describe, has had a profound impact on the spiritual lives of the members of St. Francis UMC.

Chapter 3 tells the story of the creation of Concord Presbyterian Fellowship in Delaware, Ohio, under the guidance of Pastor Ginny Teitt. Ginny, the daughter of a world-renowned evangelist, was a homemaker and mother of seven, the youngest of whom is now finishing high school, when she decided to enter seminary. When she graduated, Ginny discovered the area in which she and her family lived had been targeted by the Presbyterian Church for new church development. She was offered the opportunity to pastor the Concord Fellowship, which would then become the Concord Presbyterian Church. She spent her first summer as pastor preaching to about five dozen faithful souls outside in a tent. Now meeting in a public-school cafeteria, the congregation has more than doubled in size and the ministry of this faith-filled Christian "family" has touched innumerable hearts and lives.

Chapter 4 opens the doors of one of the most vibrant Southern Baptist churches in the country, Second Baptist Church in Houston, Texas. Dr. Ed Young is the pastor, and though Second Baptist Church has over 40,000 members and its program is equally extensive, the mission of the church is simple: "to be a Bible-teaching church, committed to sharing the promise of the Gospel with the least, the last and the lost." Members of this flourishing congregation take their commitment to Bible study seriously: volunteer teachers prepare 15 to 20 hours each week in order to instruct their classes. The members are also sincere in their desire to care for others. When the survivors of Hurricane Katrina descended upon their community, the leadership at Second Baptist Church mobilized tens of thousands of volunteers to organize and staff shelters and gathered millions of dollars to aid in the process.

Chapter 5 describes the work of Park Slope United Methodist Church located in Brooklyn, New York. The congregation's pastor, Herb Miller, has brought a profound spiritual depth to this congregation known nationwide as a voice for progressive Christianity, particularly concerning the full inclusion of gay and lesbian Christians in the life of the church. Herb clarified his call to the ministry during a silent sojourn with the Taizé Community in France following his years at Yale Divinity School. Though he has served Park Slope United Methodist Church for less than five years, Herb has been instrumental in helping this activist congregation rethink its ideas about prayer, Bible study, and worship.

2

Building Church: St. Francis United Methodist Church, Charlotte, North Carolina

Grant that I may not so much seek to be consoled as to console;
To be understood, as to understand;
To be loved, as to love;
For it is in giving that we receive....

—from the Saint Francis of Assisi Prayer

St. Francis United Methodist Church could be described as a large, single-story, brick building located about 30 minutes from the business center of Charlotte, North Carolina. But to pen an accurate portrayal of this church, the word building should be used as a verb, not a noun. Members of this congregation helped build a new home in south Charlotte and repair homes in the Gulf Coast and the Appalachian Mountains. They worked for four years to build an orphanage in central Mexico and organized numerous work teams to rebuild a church in Jamaica. Their own church structure is relatively new, completed about 12 years ago, but these committed Christians are already exploring plans to build something more on their ten-and-a-half-acre lot to accommodate their growing congregation. Though clearly each edifice, be it in Jamaica, Mexico, Appalachia, New Orleans, or Charlotte, is precious, this congregation knows that what really matters is building church.

Dividing the back of the St. Francis United Methodist Church (UMC) building down the middle, a single very wide hallway leads directly into the sanctuary. It is Sunday and the 8:30 A.M. service is under way. The sanctuary is surprisingly full, given the number of people milling around in the hall, some of whom are engaged in intense conversation. Others fill this large, comfortable space with boisterous laughter, evoking looks from the ushers welcoming latecomers to the early morning worship service. Sandy, the much loved pastor's wife, stands by the sanctuary door and waves through the window to her husband as he preaches about glimpses of paradise. He notices her, smiles a little, and keeps talking. The conversations, the laughter, and the preaching continue. Sandy walks back down the hallway to her office to prepare her children's sermon for the 10:30 A.M. service.

Sandy's office—in addition to being the pastor's wife, she is also the Director of Christian Education at St. Francis—was a topic for discussion at a recent Staff/Parish Relations meeting. It seems there are those among the faithful who were hoping that their children's education might include a more concrete connection between godliness and cleanliness. Her advocates, and they are legion, argue that it is simply not that bad: they can always find space on the floor if they need to clear off a chair. More than that, they celebrate the banners and books that cover the table and the large metal shelves that run the length of the room, filled with 50, probably more, plastic boxes of varying sizes labeled scissors, tape, markers, crayons, colored paper, and all the other building materials one might need to poke at the imaginations of the young and the used-to-be-young who wander in ready to take on the task of constructing Christian community.

Kevin, the Youth Director, works in the office two doors down from Sandy's. His space feels like a youth director's office, the walls adorned with colorful t-shirts signed by kids feeling very emotional at the end of any number of successful weekend retreats. A guitar leans against the desk, and his piles of papers and books offer silent testimony to myriad projects past and present. Together Kevin and Sandy minister to a growing number of young people *and* their families. Indeed, many adults have found their way to St. Francis United Methodist Church through their children.

DEBRA PRESSLEY

Struggling Still

Ryan Pressley was not yet 18. He had recently moved to Charlotte with his mom and dad, Debra and Hank, and his 13-year-old sister, Amanda, whom he adored. To make a little spending money and maybe save a little for college, Ryan was working part-time at Harris Teeter, a local grocery store. The Pressley family was Christian, and they had visited several churches since arriving in Charlotte. Debra was looking for a place with a good youth program, something to help keep the kids' "feet on the path." In March (1998), they visited St. Francis United Methodist Church. They went with another family whose son worked at Harris Teeter with Ryan. He kept saying to Ryan, "come on, come on." So finally, the Pressley's went. Two months after they started visiting, Ryan was killed in a car accident a few blocks from the church.

We lived just right around the corner. And he was coming home from school in another kid's car. This church—even though we'd only been here six maybe seven weeks I think was all that we'd been visiting here—it was like, "what do you need? What do you want us to do?" You know they just did everything. This church gave my daughter an anchor. Slowly but surely this church gave us—I don't have a good word for it—the base, the underpinning, the support to go on living, to go on surviving. The people here and their strong faith, just kind of, without overwhelming—I mean they didn't converge on us—it wasn't that at all; they were just here for us. And I think my husband and I just realized if we were to be able to see him again, we got to be there, too.

They had always been Christian, but now something was different. Debra and Hank have worked harder in the last eight years. It was not that they took their faith lightly before, but religion was for other purposes. They had focused more on their kids and maybe enjoyed the social aspects of the church, "you know, all the reasons people go to church."

Debra was raised Catholic. Her dad is Catholic and her mom is United Methodist. She is proud of her parents, whom she considers a real success story from their generation, because mixed marriages—and in their generation that truly was a mixed marriage—were socially unacceptable in many circles. Debra's maternal grandfather refused to attend her parents' wedding.

My dad is very devout, a strong Catholic. When they got married my mother had to agree that the children would be raised Catholic. But she told my dad, "you WILL take them to church." And he always did. There are five of us and we went to church every Sunday. We were in Catholic Youth. We were in Sunday School. We were in everything.

Her family lived in Oklahoma until she was in the sixth grade. Then her dad, an aircraft mechanic, got a job at Fort Rucker in Alabama, about a hundred miles north of Panama City; in other words, "way down South." Debra lived there until she graduated from high school. Then she moved to Atlanta, "'cause that's where the jobs were for my age group, all that kind of stuff."

As a child and later as a teenager she was always in church, so Debra had a religious foundation. But it was little more than a routine until she and Hank got married and had children. ("Just like most people...I don't know, what is that statistic when people come back to church?") Then the Pressleys really returned to the church.

Hank was raised by Baptist parents who went to the Methodist Church in the community because it was closest to their home. Debra decided that she did not want to go to a different church than her husband—though her parents still do it to this day.

They do fine. But I didn't want that for my family. So we said we don't care what the sign says out front. We don't necessarily care about the denomination; we wanted to find a place where we were comfortable. We have moved several times in our married life, and most of the time we have ended up at a Methodist church, because it has been what is most comfortable. The people at St. Francis don't just read the books and sing the hymns and stuff. It's very much a part of their lives.

It is the closeness, the gently powerful faith community, that continues to hold Debra, Hank, and Amanda. In their very brokenness they have found family. They have found family that nurtures friendships across generations and that honors those with questions and those whose lives are lived in response. It is a church family. The community at St. Francis has found the delicate balance between lovingly embracing its congregants and genuinely welcoming newcomers. Debra has experienced this firsthand and witnessed it time and time again. "Everybody—you walk in the door and you're a member. People care about you and it's not just to get you in the door. It's real and its long term." It is being a part of a group of people who are building church.

People who say I can be a Christian sitting in my backyard meditating, I don't buy that. It's a tough road to be a Christian in the United States with all the distractions we have, and all the gifts we have. I think it's harder sometimes to keep your focus where it needs to be and to be able to walk the path every day, if you don't have people that you keep close to you walking the same path.

With an age difference of just four years between them, Amanda was devoted to Ryan and he to her. Their parents have no doubt, "They were closer between themselves than they were with us. They really were." Amanda lost her brother when she was 13. For three or four years after his death, she was searching long and hard. Sometimes the path eluded her. She found—or perhaps it is more accurate to say she was found by—St. Francis United Methodist Church during that bewildering journey.

The church was good for her. A church with a larger youth group might not have been as good for her.

She got one-on-one attention, and it helped her find a place to put her feet, a path to follow. Throughout her teenage years, she very strongly identified herself with St. Francis and her Christian faith. She was a dedicated participant in the youth Bible study. When Sandy started a covenant group with the high school kids, Amanda was there. And she brought her friends, kids that did not go to church. It was not necessarily because she wanted to bring them to Christ; as with any typical teenager, it was as much about wanting her friends around as it was worrying about the state of their souls.

One of the teenage screaming fits we had, she said that she couldn't stand the sight of us any more and that Sandy was her favorite person in this world, the only important person to her in this world. And we just smiled. We just smiled and said, "Thank you. Thank you, God." 'Cause that's okay with us, let her be your favorite person in the world. That's fine with us.

There were not many theological discussions during those years. But one evening when Amanda was a senior, Debra was thinking about her son and raising some rough questions about her own faith. Amanda was the only one there, so Debra was reaching out to her.

And Amanda responded, "I never question my faith. Ma, I never question that Jesus is there for me." She was so strong in her statements to me. It took me back. It made me feel good. I was glad to hear it out of her. She was stronger in her faith than I was. Maybe that's youth or whatever, but she did come across very strong in her claim that she couldn't make it through every day without turning to God and praying. That was really something. I hope she's still there.

Shortly after Ryan's death, still searching for her own path, Debra joined a grief support group at a local Catholic church. The grief counselor who facilitates the meeting is a nun. For almost ten years, the group has been gathering together twice a month, for a meeting and then for dinner. Most of their discussions are practical, about coping and how to deal on a day-to-day basis and support each others' lives. But then there are the faith discussions. Several of the women have lost their children to cancer or other illnesses, and others have lost children to car accidents. The discussion about which is harder, which is more testing to your faith, which is tougher to recover from (not recover from but live with) is ongoing. Some who lost children so instantly imagine it would be harder to watch your child suffer, but the women who went through illness and disease wonder if the immediacy would not be harder to handle since the mother has no time to prepare, to love that child, and to talk to that child. A sick child suffers, but at least his or her mother can do the "mother thing." Debra, on the other hand, could do nothing. All opportunities to change it or fix it were gone. Each time the topic arises, resolution eludes its participants. "I don't think one is harder than the other, they're just different." The outcome aches regardless, and taking the long view has not worked for Debra.

I hate to sound like a person who's just looking at her feet, but it's a daily struggle with me. I'm just worrying about the next step—doing what I should do today. You know, every time things come at me I ask, "Is that what God wants me to do?" I feel like I'm very much a struggler. I still struggle with my faith a lot. I struggle with my faith over the loss of my son. I still struggle a lot. And my best way of keeping my focus is to do it day by day. Maybe that's different from other people. I can't look out there [into the future]. I don't see an ideal type of person, a saint type of person and say, "That's what I want to get to." I'm just trying to get through day by day.

Study groups at the church have also been some help. Her own religious education had not included much Bible study, but since joining St. Francis Debra has taken advantage of the many opportunities to do Bible study. She has done all of the Disciple Studies,[1] which has helped her develop a more personal and more informed foundation for her faith. She has begun to gather favorites, places in the Bible she likes to go....

I love Romans, and that sort of thing. I love the Proverbs. I love some Psalms, but after awhile Psalms get on my nerves. I like Ecclesiastes. I love Paul. I have a running argument with one of the members here who teaches all these Bible studies. He knows I really love Paul and he is not a great fan of Paul, so we have this constant dialogue. It's good. I have become more conversant in the Bible, and that has helped me understand so much more.

Prayer is something else all together. Some people have suggested to her that, as a result of growing up Catholic, Debra was not taught to pray freely because she prayed only structured rather than extemporaneous prayers. Debra admits that may be true. She is very uncomfortable creating her own prayers, particularly in a public setting. During her three-year tenure as lay leader of the congregation, before and after meetings, at public ceremonies or community meals, people were constantly asking her to lead them in prayer. She was convinced that she *was not good* at it, and she *did not* like it.

Now this is just me, but I find it difficult to pray. And I try real hard at it. I do more of dialogue thing, which I think is prayer, too [though there is a question in her voice]. I do have a constant dialogue with God all the time. And I think of that as prayer. I hope that's prayer. I always try to remind myself of the structure: that it's not just "keep her safe as she's driving back to Greensboro this afternoon." So I pray, but it's probably not the conventional.

Debra is clear that her dialogue with God is just that—a two-way conversation, but the subject of God's response to prayer beyond the conversation remains a tough one for her. She has heard many people say "this sickness or that illness was healed because of my prayers" or "our prayers saved him." With no intention of diminishing or dismissing those experiences, Debra describes a number of women—she may even be one of them—who just do not want to hear about that.

Because we prayed just as much, we loved our child just as much and. . . . No, they will not subscribe to the "prayer saves" idea.

Yet, she accepts that medical science, even though we wish it could, cannot fix everything. God is in control. For her this is the confusing, humbling, at times painful, reality of the human condition. She recognizes that there are people who claim a very strong prayer life and feel empowered by it.

It's a wonderful thing for them. It is. Prayer is a powerful thing, but it can be a divisive thing when people take credit for their prayers. This is one subject I can get a little touchy on.

A couple of years ago Debra went with the women of her grief support group to see John Edward. ("Not the John Edwards who is our senator in North Carolina, but the John Edward who says he can speak to the dead; the guy who has written the books."[2]) He was in Charlotte at one of the big auditoriums; the place was packed. Debra found it fascinating to see all the people who believed Edward could communicate with the dead ("and maybe he can"). But during that show, which is how she characterizes the event, she saw a lot of people hungry for a connection. Regardless of whether Edward can actually speak with the dead, what struck Debra was Edward's claim that those prayers that are accompanied by overwhelming love-filled emotions, a mother's love, for example, are heard more clearly by God because those voices are somehow louder. In her own life, when Debra talks with God about something that is really important to her, she can feel the connection. Not all the time, but sometimes it is there—often enough to keep the conversation alive and interesting.

Debra's inward spiritual journey has also led her out into the world. She and Amanda joined a work trip to Tequisquiapan, Mexico, where St. Francis United Methodist Church helped a small, local Methodist church to build an orphanage. There were a lot of young children living on the streets in this village in the northern central highlands of Querétaro. They needed a place to live and someone to care for them. This tiny Mexican Methodist church decided to build an orphanage, and the congregants of St. Francis agreed to assist them. Amanda and Debra were part of the construction team.

When we traveled from the airport to Tequisquiapan (a trip of about two hours) we passed through the Mexican countryside in what can only be described as third-world poverty. As an adult, I knew, of course, that rural Mexico was very poor, but neither Amanda nor I were prepared for the extreme poverty that we were exposed to. We also went through checkpoints at certain places. There were many military soldiers with rifles checking our papers and our bus looking for drugs.

Team members stayed in the homes of their host congregation and worked hard during their long, hot days in Mexico.

The families we stayed with were considered middle class and working families who had more than most. Their homes were poor by our standards. Some didn't have running water into the kitchen. Hot-water heaters were only turned on when you needed them. Plumbing did not allow used toilet paper to be flushed. Little things which they lived with every day and were normal life.

The team worked hard to complete the project, but it is not the blisters or the tired muscles that feature foremost in Debra's retelling of those memorable few weeks. It is the community, the simplicity, the poverty, and the generosity that she emphasizes. Having had that experience in Mexico, Debra sees the world a bit differently.

So much of the poverty in the world is due not to the people's abilities or desires, but the corruption and oppression of their rulers or governments. In Africa, South America, Central America, or the Far East those in power over the generations have taken advantage of the people to line their pockets and keep their power. Now after generations of that, even if you have a government that wants to make a difference, it is almost impossible to lift a country up out of total unindustrialized poverty. I don't have the answers.

Neither did her newfound Mexican friends, but Debra observed that they looked northward for inspiration. She listened as they compared their situation to that of the United States, and she emerged from these discussions with a renewed sense of responsibility: the United States must be made worthy of the admiration of her neighbors.

One of the things that was very clear from the people we were around in Mexico was that everyone admired the U.S. for its jobs and opportunities, but also for its laws and safety. The laws in Mexico are dependent on the local authorities. Corruption is rampant. Therefore, I have a very strong belief that the way to tackle the immigration problem is to make scrupulously sure that our laws are fair and administered evenly and quickly, but also to make sure the borders aren't just opened wide. We can't keep what makes us the place everyone wants to come if we become more and more like the country they are leaving. Our laws have to be upheld, but we have to look at our laws and make sure they are fair.

Debra is convinced that the trip was more of an education for Amanda than any amount of teaching a mother could have done. An active member of the church's mission committee, Debra would like to participate in more mission trips, but she finds it difficult to fit this into her work schedule. The church sends a group to the Gulf Coast once a month, but the week it chose is the second week of every month. Debra is an accountant for an environmental-control technology firm. She does the books for the geologists and hydrogeologists, air people, and water people. The week of the monthly Gulf Coast work trip is the week she does her billing for the whole office and she just cannot be away. Finding the balance between the need to work for her living and the desire to work in order that others might live more fully is difficult. Still, St. Francis "does mission stuff," and being a part of a mission-oriented church continues to provide a challenge, which Debra willingly, even gratefully, confronts every day.

The strong connections overseas and the deep commitment to missions do not necessarily reflect a congregation committed to political activism—liberal or conservative. Certainly people in the church can and do speak their minds. But subjects like presidential politics or the war in Iraq give Debra pause. They are rarely discussed in church.

We don't. . . . Well, I could say this different ways. It [the war in Iraq] is, it was and still is discussed, but things. . .but it's not from the political point of view. You know there aren't political comments that are brought into it by and large. It's more a discussion of what is actually going on. I think our focus has been sending boxes of stuff to. . .we had at one time either three or four, either members of this church or members' relatives whether it be a child, a sibling, or a cousin, who were soldiers in Iraq. We were sending boxes and goodie bags and whatever they needed. It's more along those lines. There has been a discussion of the current events of what is happening along those lines, but it's not, I don't want to say never, but the total focus is not the political side of it. It's more the human need, and that's what the church is here for.

Nonetheless Debra's faith shapes all her political decisions and opinions. For this thoughtful, intelligent Christian woman, though she does not converse about it in church, religion and politics are inextricably linked.

I don't know that you can separate the two. If you look back over the history of our country, there have always been very strong people of faith in power. Just go back and read the Federalist Papers and the writings of George Washington and Jefferson and James Madison. If you read the writings of the founders of our country and how they structured everything, you see the first place they turned was to God to pray. So when we look around today and people ask if it makes you uncomfortable, I say, "No, I don't find it uncomfortable." I find it odd that we would ask the question, "Do you find it uncomfortable?" I think faith should always be a part of politics.

She is comfortable, even pleased, having a president in the White House who readily acknowledges his faith.

I like the fact that Bush will pray openly, and he does not hesitate to say, even say in his speeches, "You know, I prayed about that," and he doesn't just use that as an offhand term. He does pray. He really does.

Whether you like his politics or not, George W. Bush has been true to his faith and uses his moral barometer in his leadership. I wouldn't agree with all his governing decisions, but all in all, in an extremely difficult presidency, he has kept his moral barometer. In similar difficult times, Abraham Lincoln also leaned on his moral barometer, although if he were president today, he would be impeached. He suspended civil rights, threw journalists in jail, etc. But he was in the middle of the Civil War that could have brought down our country, and he did everything he felt was necessary. Now we admire him.

I don't know why we view it so differently now that we want to separate it so much. Separation of church and state is not in the Constitution or the Declaration of Independence. Those words aren't there. It calls on us not to create a state religion. That's it. The United States should be open to freedom of religion. What you strive to have is a balance, not to expunge religion from all aspects of our life. You can't take the moral barometer out of the decisions that are made that affect the whole country. And whether it's a Methodist up there praying or whether it's a Catholic up there praying. (John Kennedy prayed. Did they go nuts? Well, yes they did. We don't remember that now. But they did. "He's a Catholic and he eats his children," that sort of thing.) It's faith that you want your leaders to have. When they make their decisions, they look at this and they look at that. They make choices about the people who will help them make choices that affect us all. It is two different things: government and faith. But I would hope that the people who are in government have a strong faith, a moral barometer. Some people just don't have a moral barometer. It would be a frightening thing if you had someone making those decisions that didn't have that faith base.

Debra admits that it is tough to determine whether or not a particular leader has that moral barometer. She analyzes actions, not just words.

You have to measure and weigh not only what a politician says, but what they do. Same way I measure anybody. Words are cheap. I always look at their background and their voting history. You have to see their record and see if he/she has been consistent. Politicians who change according to polls and current media are not to be trusted.

She also looks at issues. The one that she cares about most is freedom.

I really care about freedom—freedom of the press, freedom of religion. Your freedom goes all the way until you infringe on someone else's freedom—not just offend someone, but infringe on their freedoms. We really have become a society that believes you can't do something if it offends me. We do not have the right not to be offended. I know many laws are necessary for societal order and to give people equal chances to opportunities, but many laws and programs overstep.

I hold to the founding fathers' belief in self-reliance and less government is more freedom. Less taxes. Open marketplace. Freedom to have your own business without interference. You know, the American Dream.

Debra Pressley may be struggling still on her own spiritual journey, but this thoughtful woman certainly has found a faith-filled vision for the world in which she lives.

It is almost 10:30 A.M. Sandy leaves her office and finds her kids, Alex, 17, and Hannah, 15, and enters the sanctuary for worship. Debra and her husband, Hank, are the greeters this morning, warmly welcoming newcomers and old friends. Sandy and her family are definitely the latter. After some nods, many smiles, and more laughs, Sandy finds a place in the back corner of the sanctuary and sits down. Though she has done this hundreds and hundreds and hundreds of times before, she seems excited. Alex and a few friends sit behind her amusing themselves in unimaginable ways with the hymnal. Hannah is up front accompanying the hymns on the church's xylophone.

With windows on three sides, faux stucco and brick walls, and a high ceiling supported by beautiful exposed wooden beams, the sanctuary is filled with light. The room has comfortable movable chairs enhanced by dark maroon cushions. As this community's only gathering space, the sanctuary is used for meetings and dinners as well as worship; this is one of the things that will change when a new building is built.

The service begins with a hymn, "All Hail the Power of Jesus' Name." After the Call to Worship ("Shine in us Lord Jesus and shine forth from us") the congregation joins in prayer:

. . .At times we choose to walk in darkness, our vision obscured.
We do not care to look within,
And we are unwilling to look beyond at those who need our help.
O God, we are too weak to walk unaided.
Be with us as a strong and wise friend,
And teach us to walk by the light of your truth. . . .

Jewish Prayer for Forgiveness, USA, 20th Century

One of the teenagers has been asked to read a scripture this morning, but as he prepares to read Pastor Ben also stands, walks to the center of the sanctuary, and begins a passionate introduction to the offering. He talks about the importance of giving and of Christian formation. He tells a story about a little boy learning to pray The Lord's Prayer. Ben is inspired. He is inspiring his congregation. He opens his arms wide and looks around as if to touch each person in that sanctuary. Out of the corner of his eye, he sees a bewildered youth standing at the pulpit. Ben laughs an easy laugh, realizing he skipped the Bible passage, and says, "OK, go ahead and read." And he sits down to listen.

> ...the god of this world has blinded the minds of the unbelievers, to keep them from seeing the light of the gospel of the glory of Christ who is the image of God.
>
> (2 Corinthians 4: 4)

BEN DEVOID

Blinded Minds and Wise Friends

Ben Devoid grew up in Chicopee, a struggling blue-collar mill town in western Massachusetts. In addition to harboring Ben during his early years, Chicopee was also the proud home of the world's largest kielbasa, "which is basically a huge piece of meat." (Although the last time Ben visited, the sign had been taken down, so he is not sure if his hometown still holds the honor.) Ben recalls that the kielbasa was heavily guarded by police, since one year it was stolen. That event made national television. Chicopee hosts, or did host during Ben's childhood, an annual kielbasa festival and polka parties every Sunday afternoon. So Ben knows how to polka pretty well, a skill he rarely has occasion to share in his current role as pastor of St. Francis United Methodist Church.

The route from Massachusetts mill town to Charlotte suburb was not easy, but ease is not really something Ben ever expected from life. His mom grew up in New York City, first in Brooklyn and then in Queens. His dad grew up along the New Hampshire/Canadian border in a town called Berlin ("pronounced BER-lin"). Most kids in Chicopee were Roman Catholic. Ben was Protestant, although he has few memories of going to church.

When stories about childhood are traded, Ben just chuckles. His mother was divorced twice. She raised her four kids on a waitress's tips and the hourly income of a teacher's aide. Her second marriage was "real bad," and Ben stayed out of the house a lot during those days.

I remember when I was in high school, I had pretty wild friends. We used to take the flashers on the highway, ya know kid stuff—stupid stuff, but not really bad *stuff. I never got into a lot of trouble. I started drinking a little bit when I was 16. That was about the time I met Bill Richards.*

Ben swam in high school and some in college and, by most accounts, he did fairly well. During his sophomore year in high school he was a lifeguard in the old city pool. There was a man who would come to swim laps just when they were getting ready to close. The rule was the pool could be closed 45 minutes early if no one was in the water. Invariably the water would be still, Ben's thoughts had turned toward home, and the middle-aged man would walk through the door for his evening's exercise.

It was at that time Ben's mother had gone through her second divorce, and she wanted to find a church. Sitting in the pew one Sunday Ben looked up and the person in the pulpit of the church his mother had chosen to visit was the man he had seen swimming. "That's the guy from the pool. I didn't know he was a minister." His name was Bill Richards. He recognized Ben and the two became friends.

We became very close. He taught me to drive. He came to my swim meets. He picked me up after school now and then and took me places, like I was one of his kids. So I'm very unusual. I think part of it was he saw a kid that just really needed something—had some need, that's what it was. At some point, something inside him said, "Well, maybe I can work with him." During those high school years and freshman and sophomore college years when I commuted, he had a big hand—I could even go so far as to say—in raising me. He gave me a lot of his time. When I look back on it now, I didn't understand that then, but he was a busy man. He had four kids about my age, maybe a little younger. And there he was sort of taking in this other kid. He had a huge influence on me. I could go to his house anytime. He's the one who sent me to Pfeiffer [College]. I think he saw me—I was majoring in criminal justice—I just was really floundering. I wasn't getting into trouble, but he could tell that I didn't really have any direction. He pretty much said, "Why don't you look at this school?" It was out in the country, and he thought it would be great for me to get away.

So in 1980 Ben started as a junior at Pfeiffer College in Misenheimer, North Carolina. The school had fewer students and was more rural than Westfield State where he attended two years previously. Bill had been convinced that Ben needed something more intimate—smaller classes, somebody to watch over him to make sure he was getting focused. Ben was already toying with the idea of seminary, but he did not make that decision until he had moved south. As he had at Westfield State, Ben entered Pfeiffer as a criminal justice major. He was doing fine, planning to work in probation after graduation, which he would probably be doing today, except that he went to North Carolina without a car. Ben could not pay tuition and pay his car insurance, so he sold his car before leaving Massachusetts. When it came time to complete the off-campus placement required for the criminal justice degree, the only jobs available were out in the country. Ben had no transportation. His advisor suggested Ben had enough classes for a sociology major—and told him if he were heading to seminary it would not really matter. So Ben switched majors and headed to seminary.

My calling comes a lot from Bill. I think I watched him and I thought, "Oh, I can do that. I can do what he's doing, and I wouldn't be half bad at it." I know it sounds a little superficial [laughing], but that's what my calling is; it was that relationship. That's really how it all—I never had a real spiritual awakening. I had a friendship. It is huge and it's still always with me.

A friend, a wise friend helping to clear the path for an at least partially blinded mind, that is who Rev. Bill Richards was for Ben Devoid. Ben went directly from Pfeiffer to seminary (Candler School of Theology at Emory University in Atlanta, Georgia). "I wish I hadn't done that." But he received an academic scholarship from Candler. "Quite honestly," he admits, "I think it would have been good for me to work, but I couldn't have gotten a job where I could have paid rent and saved money to go to school. What kind of job was I going to get with a sociology degree? So I just went on and did it, because I didn't have anybody supporting me financially. I pretty much put myself through school." But Ben was no stranger to work.

I always had to work. One summer I had a job painting. I painted everything with white paint, and I always wished I had another color I could paint. The worst job I had was at this huge Episcopal Church. I did data entry, oh man, looking at that computer all day. I've had all kinds of jobs. I worked at a tobacco farm when I was in high school (in Massachusetts). I'd take a bus. I'd get up early in the morning and they'd pick up a bunch of kids [and take them to the fields in Connecticut], and I'd work on a tobacco farm going in there and doing picking. It was shade tobacco. Life guarding, I taught swimming lessons. I did a lot of that. I've had a lot of jobs. I think it was good for me. It's funny though, I wouldn't want my kids working on tobacco farms because they're really rough. Yeah, some of the things I did, I don't really want them doing. But I don't regret doing it. It gives me a sense of the world.

The summer after Ben's first year in seminary he married Sandy. They met at Pfeiffer where she was studying to be a Christian educator. Sandy joined Ben in Atlanta and began working in a local church. Ben continued his studies and worked for a professor, Adrian Carr, doing typing and filing, "grunt work." Ben loved his studies and has fond memories of his classes with Fred Cradock, Jim Hopewell, and Roberta Bondi. But he was working, so he did not get involved much in the campus community. Ben did not permit himself the luxury of engaging in those moments of soul-searching that fill the days and nights of many, particularly young, seminarians.

Honestly, I had been on survival mode for so long, that's really how I operated. I knew I had to get from one point to the other, and I was just going to do it.... I rode my bike to school, which was a bit of a ways, but I just had to get from point A to point B. I think I am still operating that way.

After seminary, point A, it was time to look for an appointment in a church, point B. The decision to stay in the South was not hard. Ben contacted the pastor of his home church, Faith United Methodist in Massachusetts. (Bill had moved on, but Ben had retained his membership in that congregation.) She would be willing to sponsor Ben for ordination, but she was candid: there were very few appointments open in the area. In fact, a number of people who had been ordained the previous year had not received appointments. Simply being practical, Ben realized "point B" was not in Massachusetts, so he kept looking.

The father of a friend from Pfeiffer was a district superintendent[3] in The United Methodist Church in North Carolina. Ben went to his house for dinner one night, met with him, and asked if he could serve a church in North Carolina. The district superintendent said, "Why not?" Having found point B, Ben and Sandy, who had grown up in northern Connecticut, would now become Southerners, sort of.

Ben's first appointment was a two-point charge: Bonds Grove United Methodist Church and Marvin United Methodist Church, neither located far from his current appointment at St. Francis UMC. With a genuine grin lighting his eyes he recalls Marvin, an old, old church with mostly old, old people. "My goal was to keep everybody awake during the service and I didn't always succeed...." Ben was new at this church stuff. And he is the first to admit that in the beginning he did not really know what he was doing.

I was nervous about it. This is how little church background I had—when I had my first church, Sandy had to help me pick out the hymns. I didn't know the hymns. I knew the hymns I had sung for those two-and-a-half years at Faith UMC, but you know I wasn't musical. I didn't grow up with hymns, and seminary doesn't prepare you for that. I had a class on worship that went over funeral services and that was good. But I had never been to a funeral. That is the honest-to-God truth. I went to a few wakes in the Catholic Church, but no, no funeral services. We didn't go to church. I just saw what Bill was doing, and I wanted to do that.

Ben's second appointment was as an associate pastor. It was not a good fit. He was much happier when he was working on his own. Thus the seven years serving a church in the Blue Ridge Mountains, his third appointment, were a delight for him and his family. Then the Bishop called in mid-May (1998) and told Ben she wanted him to talk with the people at St. Francis UMC in an upscale Charlotte suburb. They needed a minister. They could not pay their mortgage. Less than 20 years since its inception, the congregation had had a number of "false starts." The Bishop said, "That's where I really want you to go." So Ben and his family left their mountaintop and down to the suburbs they went.

Though looking at his life one could probably make a strong argument in its favor, Ben rejects the notion that the hand of God is guiding his or anyone's steps.

You know, people always say, "God is leading me to do such and such." I just look at them and think, "Aahhhhhhhh, that's really great for you to know that, but I don't think Jesus tells us the particulars in life." I know that sounds odd being a minister, but I just don't. I think the stuff we're doing is really pretty clear. I think the Beatitudes, loving one another, the parables. It's all really clear. But about whether or not I take this job or that job, I've preached on that, I don't think God cares a whole lot. It really depends on whether or not you're using those teachings and applying them to the life that you've chosen. I don't think it's like there's a play and you have a particular role. But I think it's whether or not you're willing to take on the call, take on feeding the hungry, visiting the sick.

Ben sees too many people who have struggled too hard, who have not found their way, to permit him the privilege of claiming God determines his course. "I think what God has done, through the church, is given me a home, given me a place." It is an intensely personal relationship with Jesus that affords Ben this security, this calm emerging from the chaos. He feels connected to Jesus and the edgy life that man lived. Ben loves the Gospels, especially the Gospel of Mark. There, in those pages, Ben encounters the Son of God, a teacher and a very human man. Ben relishes the Divine unafraid of getting dirty, casting out demons. Ben savors the "in your face" Jesus of the Gospel of Mark, a Jesus who gets rough and who heals real people.

I see a true divinity there in Jesus, by the way he gave himself up for the whole world. That to me is the core of the Gospel. I like people who have rough edges. I am more attracted to them. I guess 'cause that's what I grew up with.

Ben does not have a daily spiritual discipline, although he thinks he probably should. Still, he does a lot of writing and reading. He reads the Bible every day. When he was younger, he read everything Dorothy Day wrote. *The Long Loneliness*,[4] her autobiography, stands out. He is convinced that she was a true woman of God. Day's commitment to working beside working people makes absolute sense to Ben.

When I think of the great leaders of the twentieth century, their integrity came by way of being servants. They were people with exceptional vision, but never removed from the ones they longed to liberate or provoke.

Grappling with Dietrich Bonhoeffer, another theologian who was "really down and dirty," helped Ben construct his worldview.

I don't necessarily think the Kingdom coming means that everyone will be a Christian, or at least I'm not sure that is the intention. Could it be that God has chosen to manifest Himself in different ways to different worldviews, or different cultures? That said, when John says that Jesus is the Way, the Truth, and the Life, I believe it. Jesus' way of witness is the only way that will save this world from self-destruction: turning the other cheek, praying for those who persecute us, feeding the hungry, eating with the sinner, and offering grace. Isn't evangelism about inviting people to join us in such a life?

Lately Ben has been reading the work of the Most Rev. and Rt. Hon. Rowan Williams, the Archbishop of Canterbury, and Karen Armstrong.[5] Armstrong describes herself as a "freelance monotheist," and this thoughtful, compassionate, rough-around-the-edges pastor has been taken with her "real honest to goodness search." He finds himself there sometimes as well. In addition to his reading, Ben also keeps a journal.

I've been journaling since my senior year in high school. Not every day. I have a journal at my desk. I write prayers. I write my thoughts and I write to God. I always feel bad when people tell me to pray for something. I am not a good intercessory pray-er. But I talk to God a lot. I talk to God in my study. I talk to God through writing, all the time. So I do that. But I'm not a person who wakes up at 5:30 A.M. for devotions. I do swim. I've been doing that for years. (I took a break for awhile because I got really sick of it.) I do a lot of my thinking then. I do praying as well. Three thousand meters takes me about an hour, and it does really good things for me.

Personal reflection may feed his soul, but bringing in the Kingdom by sitting in church meetings makes Ben a bit crazy. "I don't like sitting in meetings. I get bored. And they know I get bored, because I leave them sometimes. I do. I just let them work it out. Somebody said to me, 'you have to stay *a little* longer!'" He laughs loud and long. He feels the same way about political work.

The political thing to me, it's uh, you know, I don't really care. Or maybe what I am trying to say is that I'm not interested in the church gaining political power, not in the sense that government has power. Our role is to call into question all politicians, regardless of party. Our allegiance is to no state, but to the cross. I really don't like the American flag in the church. It was a battle I lost in my church, and there it sits. (I am actually a bit of a political junkie, although my retention is fairly limited.)

I think our first identity as Christians is our baptism. And everything works out from there; that's how we make our decisions. If we claim Christ in all our decisions and in our relationships, then that has to be how we make our decisions. But the big challenge for Christianity is that if we claim our baptism, sometimes we have to work with what we really wouldn't want but what would be best for others. It's hard. It's real hard. Sometimes it means self-denial.

My baptism informs my decisions in the voting booth, which sometimes work against my self-interest, for example, choosing a candidate that may raise county taxes to improve decaying inner city schools. Sometimes it makes people mad. People want to be comfortable.

Ben does not judge that desire for comfort. In fact, he shares it, but he also is keenly aware that comfort can be elusive, even dangerous, and sometimes the comfort of others comes first. For Ben building church is a ministry dedicated to building a community of Christians who do not just sit around asking why people do not have adequate housing or enough to eat, although at times he wonders if he should do a little more of that.

I've done a lot to motivate groups in the church to get involved with organizations that serve the poor and addicted such as Habitat for Humanity, addiction shelters, homeless shelters, and such. But mostly these have not dealt with systemic issues—the causes. I do Dorothy Day only half way. The articles she wrote for *The Catholic Worker* were remarkable. It was her voice in the world, the other half of her ministry that I find myself missing. Would she have been as free if she were clergy? Or with some Catholic order?

It may have its limitations, but Ben's ministry is about getting up and going out into the world—answering the call by working for others. Ben is not bored by mission. This restless pastor has enthusiastically guided the congregation at St. Francis UMC as they fulfill their commitment to "carry the cross of Jesus into the world."

Every year there is at least one opportunity for congregants to leave south Charlotte and give of themselves for a week or more in some kind of mission. The point is not that some other community needs food, a house repaired, or its church floor fixed, although it does. The point is spirituality: an enriched spirit and a closer understanding of Christ and of those who are less fortunate.

The mission teams are able to accomplish a surprising, at times shocking, amount of work during their brief trips. (Ben recently took a job inventory test that revealed he was much better suited for the construction industry than the ministry.) But the benefits of these trips are not unilateral. When the sojourners return, they are "just a better church. I see less pettiness. They know what matters. I see more willingness to study the scriptures."

But the lessons learned are complicated. Ben knows the difference between doing for and working with those in need. He has witnessed, even experienced, the tendency to romanticize poverty; and so Ben the laborer, Ben the pastor, Ben the teacher, gently, masterfully encourages these well-meaning workers to take a second, or a third, look at where they are, who they are with, and what it might mean to each of them as a person of faith.

I have to be really careful. Last year we redid the floor of a church in Jamaica. It's really a very, very poor area. One of the things people would say is, "They have it all because they have each other." My response was, "Well, I'm sure if you wanted to stay, and give them your plane ticket, they'd come right over to south Charlotte, no problem." But I do feel like you see the face of Christ in the suffering. I know that I have. That's been when I've felt closest to what the Body of Christ is about. That doesn't necessarily mean they have to be poor, when I've been with people who are in trouble with the law it's been the same way. I just really do believe in that whole thing with Jesus that the last will be first and the first will be last. I really do believe that stuff. If there's anything I believe, I probably believe in that more than the bodily resurrection. I believe that you discover what the Body of Christ is when you're with part of the suffering of the Body. Which doesn't mean you're looking for suffering, it just means that's where it's at. Of course that's my real struggle here, because the whole point here is to be comfortable.

...You know I say all that, but let me tell you, at the same time it's nice to have a job where I have insurance, a decent home, a good school for my kids. Boy, is it nice to have because there were times when I was growing up where I just really did not—my mother waitressed with four kids—I just really did not have it. And I worked. Being the oldest boy, I was always concerned, always on the edge. So I say that, but boy, it's nice having a house. I don't own it, but it's nice to live in it. It's not like I was one of those kids in Jamaica..., but I've been there to a certain degree.

Ben's profound sense of gratitude for the goodness of his life continues to fuel his desire to share his abundance with all people and to urge others to do the same. When someone is in need, Ben believes his church is called to help. It is that simple. He has little patience for those who complicate matters.

One thing I struggle with in The United Methodist Church—in all the mainline churches—is that so much time is spent struggling with so much of this other social stuff, who's in and who's out. If somebody wants to help, fine, bring them in. What does it matter? The rest is a side issue.

Our identity is developed out of our baptismal covenant and our obedience to it, which is first and foremost an obedience to love. That is my struggle with the church on the gay issue. If you have claimed your baptism, your sexual orientation is secondary. I am not first a straight man; I am first a man that has chosen to follow Jesus. And that puts me into the church, not attraction to the opposite sex, or to the same sex for that matter.

Pontificating about family values consumes very little, if any, of Ben's pastoral agenda. Interruptions from his own family, however, are warmly welcomed throughout his busy week. For Ben, meeting Sandy was finding the calm in the midst of the storm.

Sandy's the most stable thing I've ever had. Her family's very stable. Gosh, they define stability. They still live in the same house. They still have the same lunch box they had when she was four, sitting on the same place on their shelf. Nothing changes. It's just the way it is.

Ben and Sandy have tried to create a Christian home for their two children, Alex and Hannah. Grace is said before each meal. Ben read the Bible to the kids when they were younger. They go to youth group. They were both confirmed. At the time of their confirmation the teenagers agreed to accept Christ and the church. It is Ben's fondest hope that confirmation "opened a door for his children to continue on that journey." Hannah and Alex identify themselves as Christians. Sometimes they even comment on their dad's sermons. "They tell me either I need to make them shorter, or they didn't understand what I was talking about." There have not been many theological discussions inspired by their father's preaching in the Devoid household.

A lot of the talk with Alex is about sports and music. I haven't talked to him about theological stuff. I guess I'm not very in tune with their spirituality [laughing]. I don't think either one wants to be a minister though; I know Alex doesn't. Alex is Alex. He doesn't like singing hymns and stuff like that. I think it's just him. Maybe someday he will.

For Ben and Sandy the walk has always been more important than the talk, or in the case of Alex and Hannah one might say the run, since both kids are exceptional high-school athletes. Regardless of the speed, the road has taken some difficult turns in last few years. Hannah was ten years old when she was diagnosed with type 1 diabetes. Before her condition was identified, she ended up in the hospital for awhile. Those were tough times for the family. When she returned home Ben had to give her insulin shots until she got used to doing it herself. Now her condition is stable, and Hannah has become a passionate advocate for stem-cell research and an active fund-raiser for the Juvenile Diabetes Research Foundation.

At about the same time Alex was floundering at the local high school. "I knew I had to get him out because he was just in a bad situation." The decision was made that Alex would enter an Episcopal boarding school up in the mountains. "One of the hardest things I ever had to do was dropping off Alex at boarding school. I didn't want to do it."

Alex reluctantly left his life-size cardboard cutout of President George W. Bush at home. But Sandy makes sure W. still feels included in the family by allowing him to welcome overnight visitors in the guest room. And Alex comes home for weekends now and then and immediately George Bush springs into action. . . . like the time when Hannah, who had gone to bed early, needed to take a bathroom break in the middle of the night. She opened her door into the dark hallway and found herself face to face with "the most powerful man on earth." One wonders if the neighbors are still puzzling over the terrifying howl followed by, "MOM, GET GEORGE BUSH OUT OF HERE."

Ben may tire easily of circuitous discussions, be they political or otherwise, but he would be the first to contend that some things do need to be said, over and over again.

It's as important for me to tell my kids that I love them as it is to ask them if they prayed before they went to bed. I think that's what they want to hear from me. I always make sure to tell them I love them, and I always try to show them affection. That's really important to me. A lot of times you do what you do because of what you didn't have. I didn't have that, so it's real important for me to give it to them. If you didn't have a parent or you felt like they just sort of took off on you, that is something you never recover from. It's always there. I operate out of that all the time.

Maybe that is why relationship—with Jesus as personal Lord and Savior, with a lap-swimming pastor, with a vibrant, visionary wife, and two very precious teenagers, wise friends each in their own way—is tantamount to a call from God for this Northern-born, Southern-bound pastor.

JIM CARTER

Hypocrites Belong in Church

Jim Carter was sitting alone in church this morning. His wife, Leslie, was at home honoring the Creator by creating some masterpieces of her own. She was making the final preparations for an upcoming art exhibition. Jim was without his wife, but he was not lonely. His booming voice could be happily heard engaged in lively conversation at the end of the service. He was certainly not the first to leave the sanctuary and head for the parking lot that Sunday morning.

There are few at St. Francis UMC who are not acquainted with Jim. For most, the mere mention of his name elicits affectionate yet artful smiles. Jim is one of those people who somehow seem to double the attendance at any event as soon as he walks through the door. He is refreshingly authentic. Without apology, he simply is who he is. Yet this intelligent, Charlotte-born lawyer is not simple. A bit like a thousand-piece jigsaw puzzle, the picture is right there on the box. But Jim Carter is honest enough to realize that life, especially his, is riddled with contradictions. The pieces do not always fit together the way one might expect.

I will be 60 years old on March 11 of this year [2006]. I am a Democrat in a sea of rich Republicans. Suburban Charlotte more and more is becoming fairly Republican. As I get older I feel like I am becoming more liberal compared to the folks I live around. I am not sure if that means I am moving left or if the folks are moving right. When I say liberal, I kind of laugh and make other folks laugh, because I have fun calling myself a left-wing liberal. I am probably more moderate. . . .

I've wondered how in the world in the '60s the religious liberals were the political folks and now the conservatives seem to have the religion banner. I don't quite understand that. The right-wing conservative Christians are doing a good job. They have been so loud and aggressive that we think our version of Christianity is not valid, or unpatriotic. We are afraid to take positions that are unpopular. What about a march for peace? Against capital punishment? Or at least against capital punishment being unevenly used? Or for fair wages? Or against commercial expatiation? Where are we on these issues?

I feel much more comfortable with the work of Martin Luther King and all those folks with the civil rights movement using Christianity in that way, than when a conservative church uses Christianity to support the war. . . .'cause I think the conservative church is wrong is the thing.

Jim has lived all his life in the South. Born and raised in Charlotte, he left the area briefly during a stint in the air force and to attend college at the University of Georgia and returned after he completed his law degree at Campbell Law School in eastern North Carolina. His location, though anyone from the South knows that is only a small part of being Southern, has profoundly shaped the way he views the world.

I kind of separate folks out sometimes. I have prejudices, and I don't know if it's because I am a human or because I am a Southerner, but I tend to be lazy and want to put folks in categories. That makes it easier for me to judge all of them. I find myself occasionally with racial sorts of assumptions.

Sorting through the pieces in anticipation of assembling the puzzle that is Jim Carter's life, one finds that pieces related to race occupy much of the table. Reconciling the social, economic, and political contradictions posed by racial diversity has been one of the most troubling paradoxes in Jim's life. As a child, segregation was essentially a given. His father died when he was four, so his mother went to work as an accountant. The Carter family had "a black lady," Lucile, who arrived at their house early in the morning, fixed breakfast, and got Jim off to school.

She was a maid. That's what we called her; that's what she was. There was just no thought around my household, no conversation about blacks or Negroes or white people or anything. It simply was a nonissue.

Jim realized that Lucile's skin was a different color than his. But that was the extent of it, until one day he was in downtown Charlotte at Sears. He saw water fountains labeled "colored" and "white."

I can still see it. I know exactly where in that building (that building's still there, but it's been changed to the county building) that thing was on the wall.

For Mrs. Carter, concerning herself or her family with the social and cultural commotion that was beginning to envelop much of the country never crossed her mind. Her unambiguous focus was on survival: she needed to make a place for her son. Jim recalls his mother as a young woman who was "very stable, almost unemotional." There was little religious participation in the Carter home and nothing that would remotely resemble the political. As a youth Jim was "a lump. I was apolitical. I was a-anything."

In spite of having painted his portrait in this way, complexities and contradictions begin to emerge through the staid, somewhat prosaic, veneer of Jim Carter's childhood. Jim is a product of the public school system. He attended Myers Park High School, "a real preppy, fairly affluent high school. We had one black there. And I don't recall any—I'm sure he felt it differently—but from my side I didn't notice him, one way or the other. He was just kind of there." Jim was surrounded by white students. He was not friends with the one black teenager in the school, but over 40 years later, Jim remembers that this young man, like himself, was a graduate in the class of 1964.

As Jim reconstructs the youth portion of his life's puzzle, his most vivid religious memory probably could be grouped with the race pieces. He was raised in a moderate Baptist Church.

When I was about 16 years old, I was invited to sit on whatever it is the Baptists have—it's not the trustees or the administrative council—the board or whatever it is. This group actually discussed whether or not they should actively solicit blacks to come to the congregation. We were fairly moderate and the consensus was, "Sure we certainly should." But there were a couple of folks that said they didn't think that was appropriate. My recollection is I was quite surprised that there was any discussion about that at all. I probably used that as an excuse to stop going to church.

In his "lumpy, apolitical, a-anything" way Jim took a stand and took his leave not only from the Baptist Church, but from organized religion. Coming to terms with religion had often led Jim as a child, a youth, and now as a mature adult to some places of profound contradiction.

As a child, Jim sometimes cried himself to sleep, mourning the loss of his father in ways only a child can understand. He blamed God, whom he did not know, for his father's death.

High school presented more challenges. Jim had a learning disability. "I was attention deficit before they knew the word. Then they just thought I wasn't trying." He had to attend summer school in order to graduate. Jim's high school struggles were not just academic. He was painfully insecure. "I had an incredible void, because I needed a dad. Also I was in an affluent high school, and I wasn't affluent. I was just a fish out of water." Recognizing the vital part played by the church during his son's teenage years merely underscores the absence of any religious support during his own youth. Jim believed that God was somehow responsible for him, especially responsible for all that he was convinced was wrong with him, but that was where the relationship ended. There was no comfort, no spiritual guidance. "I didn't find what I needed in the church—which was security and some male role models."

After high school, Jim served in the air force for almost four years (1965–1969). Part of that time he was in Germany. Then he went to Thailand. In Thailand he did electronic work on airplanes that bombed Vietnam. Though the poetry of his assertion seemingly escapes him, Jim claims that somehow he became grounded during his time in the air force. In the midst of war he made peace with the person he was and would become. "I finally realized there was some standard that I needed to measure up to that had nothing to do with other individuals."

The church and religion had little to do with this personal, empowering discovery. In fact, Jim does not remember his years in the military service as being particularly challenging spiritually. He spent little time in prayer and rarely, if ever, felt the absence of a sustaining faith. His one "religious memory" from his time in Thailand is as disturbing (to him) as it is uncomplicated.

We were on the flight line. It was Christmas Day. We had chalk and we were marking all the bombs "Merry Christmas." Then a chaplain came riding up on his bicycle.

Looking back, Jim acknowledges the numbness, the requisite insensitivity, that survival in that situation demanded. It was not as if his God had abandoned him, because for Jim, God was never really there. After completing his military service Jim went to the University of Georgia. He chose the school "because they had a good radio station and pretty girls." It was there he met his future wife, Leslie, and it was there that "at some point" Jim's "consciousness started raising."

I started buying music, Jefferson Airplane and Cream and all those kind of folks. Then Kent State happened. We marched and stuff like that. Yeah, I got a little involved, not in the higher levels of protest, but I got involved in protests. It became obvious to me that Vietnam was wrong. Being over there I hadn't given it much thought, even when I saw bombs going out. When I finally became political, it was clearly antiestablishment. I guess that's the '60s kind of thing, but it stuck.

It was four or five years into their marriage before Leslie and Jim found their way to church. In the meantime, on his own Jim had found places for a number of those "religion puzzle pieces," figuring out what God wanted of him without the "help of any religion." But as he has continued to make connections in his own life, Jim has come to appreciate the importance of gathering as a part of a faith community.

I like to be with people of faith and I enjoy other faith experiences. I almost hate that I believe in Jesus because I really enjoy synagogues. I really like Jewish tradition. They bring a Torah out—those things go back a long way. That's the real deal. And I really hate it that we Christians work so hard to separate ourselves from our Judaism past. Gimme a break, Jesus did all this stuff, but we don't do any of it. Even though I came to at least an ethical position without the help of any organized religion, I think now that a body of believers is important to be with regularly just kind of to boost you up a bit.

Ironically, given his own spiritual formation, Jim is quite skeptical of those whose pursuit of the Divine does not include organized worship. Not only community, but discipline has become vital to Jim's understanding of faith.

Oh, it's Sunday morning, I'll just look out the window and think about God. Well, there are very few of us that find God in the funny papers, although I'm sure He's there somewhere. But that's usually what we do on Sunday morning if we don't go to church. So I guess just the discipline of going to church is important even though you don't agree with everything.

There have been points in his life when the inconsistency and contradictions of the institutional church bothered Jim a lot. Then he realized "that the hypocrisy I saw in the church is exactly where it ought to be." He is convinced the church ought to be for sinners. When he was young and idealistic, the hypocrisy had pushed him away. Whether or not it was labeled racism, he certainly had not witnessed the loving compassion of Jesus. He reacted strongly and turned away from the church for a long time. He admits, "That was obviously very immature Christian theology. Of course, I was an immature kid."

Jim and Leslie returned to Charlotte when Jim started practicing law. They visited a number of churches, but chose to join Covenant Presbyterian Church, a big, beautiful stone church in downtown Charlotte.

A lot of the bankers and those kinds of folks went there. I guess we were drawn to it by the people and the facilities. It's huge, cathedral-like. The music is very traditional, wonderful choir. You really felt like it was an experience when you walked in the door. We made good friends in the Sunday School class.

The couple left Covenant Presbyterian Church when Harrison, their only child, turned ten and it became obvious that he wanted to be more involved in a church youth group. Covenant was too far away since the Carters had moved farther from the center of town. St. Francis UMC made logistical sense. The youth program was new, but it was growing. They especially liked Ben's straightforward preaching, and Sandy, according to Jim, "she shines from the inside." The Carters joined St. Francis sometime in the mid-1990s.

Some of the church folks at St. Francis took Harrison under their wings. According to his admiring father, Harrison is a "real individual." He tried on his different personalities at St. Francis. And not only did the congregation let him explore a bit, the older folks and younger folks alike genuinely seemed to enjoy and appreciate Harrison. One day his teenage son came home and said, "Daddy, this church is where I can be myself."

By the time Harrison was born, his parents were confirmed liberal Democrats convinced that "public school was kind of where it's at." But when Harrison reached school age, his parents chose a private school. The "public school piece" seemed like it should fit, but it just did not. "It was a real struggle for us. . . . Unfortunately in our community the only seeds we have had of integration have been within our public schools. We as a group have, well, look at me, I am living in the suburbs, you know it is rather hypocritical." When he was still very young, Jim and Leslie believed there was something unique about Harrison. They wanted the best education for their son. Like all good parents, they wanted "to equip him for whatever he wanted to do." Overcoming their ethical angst, they selected Charlotte Latin School, one of the older private schools in the area. (A radical desegregation program instituted in Charlotte in 1969 meant that most school children, black and white, would no longer attend neighborhood schools. The Charlotte Latin School was founded in 1970.) After visiting a number of schools the Carters were favorably impressed that Charlotte Latin School made some efforts to attract U.S. minorities and foreign students, so the student body "was not lily-white." Their son would be well educated, and his liberal parents would find a way to make two apparently incongruous "pieces" fit together.

Charlotte Latin kind of had its own style. It was the polo shirts, kind of preppy. As a teenager Harrison decided that wasn't quite who he was. He wore black collar shirts while everybody else wore pinks and blues. He tried that at church first. It worked for him, so that's who he became in school.

Jim has become a vital part in the youth ministry at St. Francis UMC. His initial involvement was prompted by the need to serve as a chaperone for Harrison. Now that Harrison is in college, Jim remains connected because working with the teenagers brings him pure joy. He also has taken on the job as chair of the church's Staff/Parish Relations Committee, the group that oversees all personnel matters of the local church. Ironically the man who abandoned organized religion when his fledgling faith could not tolerate revelations of religious hypocrisy was now to find himself as one of the primary guardians of the institution itself. And racial inclusivity, the issue that drove him from the church so long ago, still remains an unfulfilled dream, though perhaps Jim's reaction to this dilemma has seasoned with age.

Under the guidance of Pastor Ben Devoid, St. Francis UMC has developed a relationship with a local African Methodist Episcopal Zion Church (AMEZ).[6] The two congregations gather for joint worship a few times each year. While Jim enthusiastically supports these efforts, he has his suspicions about any long-term impact these gatherings might have on the daily life of his Christian brothers and sisters. His honest assessment, the only kind that Jim can offer, is that there is very little in the way of genuine relationship shared between these sister congregations.

When we have services together, everybody feels very comfortable. The people who go, and that is not a large percentage—I guess it kind of varies depending on where it is and what time it is, seem comfortable with the different styles. Nobody rushes out after the service. I don't see that at all. So, maybe I'm being a little bit harsh. Maybe there's a potential there. But I don't think we have any relationship now except just kind of getting together for services occasionally. It's kind of like an emulsion that you can shake up and it's ok for a couple of hours, but then it starts separating out. And that's what happens, real quick.

Though bemoaning the accuracy of the claim that Sunday morning worship remains the most segregated hour of American life, Jim recognizes that St. Francis UMC does indeed have a number of black members who attend regularly. He thinks of one gentleman in particular who is "totally integrated, but then, of course, he's an engineering type." This makes sense to Jim since he maintains that Charlotte is segregated primarily by economics. He claims Charlotte will accept anybody "if they're willing to tow the line, and I don't mean racial line, I mean business line."

Harvey B. Gantt was our first black mayor. Harvey's a great guy. But basically the question really is, "How pro-business are you?" That's really much more important than what color you are. I guess it's a different master. I think in a lot of ways we're reasonably color-blind.

Jim acknowledges that organizational inconsistency, what he might label hypocrisy, abounds in the church. And yet he has made peace with this. The church has become an integral part of his life. But the institutional component notwithstanding, at the heart of Jim's faith is a very personal relationship. He is absolutely convinced that God is with him "all the time." Talking is not quite adequate to explain how Jim relates to God. "That's almost too far away; He's just right with me."

In Sunday School people say they need to hear from God. I say, "Look, God's not only knocking on the door, He's trying to kick it down. Our problem is we don't open the door. It's not hard. You just have to open it."

Humility prevents Jim from declaring that he has fully opened his own door. He sighs, "That would be presumptuous. I'll let God decide that. I just feel like God's always with me." Though Jim is completely secure in his relationship with God, there is no trace of arrogance. He knows he could do more to nurture his connection to his Maker, but he is realistic about accomplishing that task.

I read some mystery book by a Christian author. Part of it was a description, I was going to say, of a retired nun, but they don't do that, do they? It was a Christian woman who had a prayer closet in her house. It had a small window and a bench and nothing else. I thought to myself, "Wow, that's pretty cool!" But I've never tried it. That's probably one of my few regrets, but it's not...but I probably don't regret it so much that I am going to change it.

As one might expect from any well-educated lawyer, Jim Carter thrives on spirited conversation. He enjoys discussing the Bible "because I enjoy discussing most anything." But complex theological paradigms do not work for him. Though he makes no reference to the passage, his "theology" could be summed up in one verse of scripture: God is love (1 John 4:7–8).

I really am just simple. I think we tend to overcomplicate what we read in the Bible. I think Bible study is highly overrated. Isn't that awful? Isn't that terrible? What God wants us to understand is that He loves us. If we understand that He would give His Son to us, what else do we need to know? It seems like all this other stuff is helpful, explanatory, supportive, and that's fine, but if you really get that God loves us and that nothing we can do will supplant his grace, that's the most important thing.

We humans have spent so much time and effort trying to make God, to bring God down to our size. By even talking about Him, I just said "Him." All of a sudden I have restricted God. I guess I think it's rather presumptuous for me to make assumptions about God. I don't understand God. I can't ever understand God. Why do we have to put Him in a white beard and a robe? It just seems incredibly diminishing of God. I think we had it right when we couldn't speak the name of God. Maybe if we didn't speak the name of God, we'd be less likely to talk about God using our puny little language.

That being said, there are times when Jim believes it is imperative that Christians find and use their voice.

Most of us are way too quiet. I tell people I'm a militant liberal. It gets their attention. In Sunday School, when I have laid it out there, whether it's about homosexuality or anything else, it's kind of surprising. It gives other folks the strength to agree. Once you say it, what's the worst they can do to you? Thank goodness, in the United States they're not going to shoot you. I am so appreciative of that. Some parts of the world they might.

He is convinced that liberal Christians are way "too careful." They are reluctant to inflict or push their religion on somebody else. "We liberals are much more careful about that than other folks. We need to become much more aggressive. We are being too politically correct and saying we'll accept anybody doing anything. We're not going to judge anybody." As a person of faith, Jim feels called to change the world, though he acknowledges that he and many others have woefully neglected this task.

We have been very inactive and very timid. Jesus was not particularly timid. Jesus was rather aggressive, and the folks he was most aggressive with were not the prostitutes, or the sinners, the bad people. He was aggressive with the power structure, with the establishment, and the ones who were in authority. Jesus was extremely political in that way.

Though some might be intimidated or overwhelmed by the daunting prospect of changing the world, Jim is not one of them. There is no reason to wait for something profound. Jim sees what needs to be done and believes it would take only minimal effort to get started.

The goal is to practice justice and fairness. It does not take too much work. As individuals we should not wait for the next big chance to make a difference. We need to practice our beliefs in the little stuff. Maybe we should call this the little-stuff movement. If we start here, it will spread. Be conscious of where we buy our socks.

Do we really want to support a slave mill in China?

Do we want to support Wal-Mart, which pushes so hard for the low wholesale price that the suppliers cut corners with safety and wages?

How do we do our jobs? Do we cut moral corners? Are we an example to others?

Do we cut off another driver just to get ahead in bumper-to-bumper traffic?

Do we keep the extra change when the clerk miscounts?

Do we speak up when someone makes a racial or sexist joke?

Do we bother to read about the political candidate and go to the trouble to vote?

We need to practice justice in our immediate surroundings. Jesus did pretty good and he talked to a relatively small number of people.

Today's church should be leading the way on some of these things, "no question about it. If we don't, who will?" Jim asks with a big, almost boyish smile.

I think that's what we're here for. The only way *God does* anything is through us. It's that old joke about this guy who hears on the radio that the flood is coming, so he says, "Okay, fine, I'll wait for God." Then the water comes up (I forget how this goes) to the second floor and a boat comes by and says we're here to save you, and the fella says, "No, God will take care of me." The water gets higher and the man gets up on the roof and they come by in a helicopter and throw a line down, and the fella says, "That's okay. God will provide." And so he drowns and he's up in heaven and he sees God, and says, "God, why didn't you save me?" And God says, "You idiot, who in the world *do* you think sent the weatherman and the boat and the helicopter?"

If I believe other folks are showing me God, I have to hope that somehow I am showing God to other people in some small way by the things I do and the things I say. So I don't think God is going to end the war, but as a Christian, if I believe the war is wrong, then I believe it is my duty to act on that belief. I don't think God wants me to say, "Okay, I'm a Christian and therefore this is what's right and wrong for you." But I think God does want us to step out a little bit and be braver than we are, knock over a few tables.

Jim Carter has a genuine commitment to knocking over a few tables of the establishment, of those in authority, of the power structure—a power structure in which people not only like him, but he himself—well off, white, Southern men—hold the power. The puzzle pieces seem like they would not fit, but the completed picture on the outside of the box indicates otherwise.

When Ben finished preaching he moved the wooden lectern, which held his handwritten notes, off to the side to clear the way for Caitlin Purcell. A sophomore in high school, Caitlin is an Irish step dancer, and the congregation delighted in watching as she shared her gifts.

> I danced in the morning when the world was begun,
> And I danced in the moon and the stars and the sun,
> And I came down from heaven and I danced on earth.
> At Bethlehem I had my birth.
> Dance, then, wherever you may be;
> I am the Lord of the Dance, said he.
> And I'll lead you all wherever you may be,
> And I'll lead you all in the dance, said he.

Lord of the Dance (United Methodist Hymnal)

The congregation sang as Caitlin moved back and forth across the front of the sanctuary. She danced for all five verses of the contemporary hymn, and when it was over she was tired, but smiling. Her father watched proudly from his place in the congregation. Dan Purcell had not had to usher today. The youth had taken care of that, but he did have to count the offering after the service. And later in the afternoon, he would bring his kids back to church for youth group.

PENNY AND DAN PURCELL

Bringing Back a Little Piece

The Purcell family is any pastor's dream. They help out. They do what needs to be done, happily, whether the task is taking out the trash, dancing in church, or organizing a mission trip. They give generously of themselves—parents and kids alike. Dan frequently ushers for the 10:30 A.M. service. His 12-year-old son, Matthew, has been joining him lately. Matthew holds the door open as people come in to worship. The other day when Dan was vacuuming the sanctuary, he turned around to find his son sliding the chairs out of his dad's way.

Penny's mom was at church all the time when she was young, and Penny would tag along. Her kids are being raised the same way. Dan is amused: "If I have a meeting down at the church, my kids want to come, even if it's an empty church."

Though their lives are centered around the church, discussions about faith are rare. Their children just do not talk about their faith much.

You know they really don't. I have a daughter who keeps a lot inside of her, and I wish she didn't. She's not really one to ask a lot of questions. My son really isn't either. I guess neither one of them is. He's doing confirmation right now. I think that would be a prime time for him to be asking questions or bring it up if he wanted to talk, but he really doesn't. I may ask him, "What did y'all talk about in confirmation?"...I hope and pray they know they can come to us. But the ages they are right now—high school and middle school—those are just tough years. I guess the bottom line is, no, they don't really communicate with us about their faith, but we take little nuggets when we can. [Penny]

Dan and Penny realize that after about three words, the kids will "tune them out." But both parents notice that their teenagers are always watching, so these wise, realistic parents try to let their actions speak for them. Family devotions have not been too successful. They have tried every now and then, especially during Lent and Advent. "It goes over pretty well," Penny reflects, "but it gets pretty silly at our dinner table, so sometimes it's kind of hard to be serious."

There may not be some elaborate spiritual regimen in the Purcell household, but the Christian message is loud and clear. Penny does not work outside the home. Her focus "for now" is on the children.

My path is sort of geared to helping them know that there's a God who loves them. Dan and I love them dearly, but our love is nothing compared to His love. We are trying to mold them enough to know when they leave us and go out into the world, college or wherever, that we won't be there, but they can have the love that God has for them with them all the time. I am just trying to lay a good foundation. What they choose to do from here is their own choice. But I'm trying to kind of at least lead them in the right way. [Penny]

Often Penny and Dan feel isolated from other parents. They both grew up with the church as the focus of their lives and the lives of those around them. Today acquaintances imply that the Purcell family is "missing something" by spending so much time at church and that they have become "stick-in-the muds" unable to enjoy themselves. Drinking, particularly teenage drinking, is an ever-present issue.

Some people say, "I'm going to have my 16-year-old drink in my house because he's going to drink anyway." But why don't we teach our 16-year-old that you don't have to drink in order to have fun? If you do that, then you're a prude and you're not being realistic. Well, wait a minute, what's realistic? Penny and I feel like we were born 30 years too late. Our children are being bombarded with you gotta drink to be cool or you gotta have this car to be cool. We feel like we're fighting the devil in a way. [Dan]

They worry that their children are receiving two very different sets of signals: one from "the world" and one from their family. They see other families who attend church when it does not conflict with their soccer schedules: families whose priorities are so different from the ones with which Penny and Dan were raised and are trying to share with their children. They see churches trying to attract new members by adapting to and even embracing "worldly values." Dan objects to these new "come-as-you-are-and-bring-your-coffee" kind of churches. For him "church is supposed to be a set-apart time, a little more reverent. Maybe in that regard we are kind of old-fashioned."

Sometimes we feel a little bit like we're under attack. You know I have a 12-year-old son who I can't hardly take to a professional football game because he's inundated with beer and scantily clad women. They say, "Oh, that's the world and you got to get used to it, you got to come around to it." Well, maybe that's the world you live in. As parents we struggle with that. [Dan]

Penny and Dan grew up in the same hometown, Asheville, North Carolina; were high school sweethearts; went to the same college, University of Tennessee at Knoxville; and then got married. "We're pretty boring." Married "20-some years," they realize it is rare to find that kind of courtship and romance these days, and Penny insists, "I definitely wouldn't want it for my two children. I just think the world's different now." And, anyway, Penny and Dan Purcell are not like most other people.

We are different than most people. I'm just a kind of a homebody, kind of simple. I didn't feel the need to get out and see the world and do all that kind of stuff. I don't think he did either. We just kind of happened to be two, I don't know if we're lazy or what, but we're just kind of soul mates. [Penny]

Penny and Dan feel blessed that they share the same faith commitments and core beliefs. Penny was raised in the church where her father's family was raised. People in her home church were not transient as they are in Charlotte, where people are always coming and going and "there's a different kind of feel." She enjoys remembering that beloved old building, which gave her such a strong sense of place.

It was a beautiful church, a beautiful, beautiful church. They just don't build them like that anymore. It had beautiful stained-glass windows, a pipe organ, and big wooden arches. When I went to church I just always felt like it was special. Church was pretty much the center of my life. [Penny]

Penny has fond memories of some of the old hymns like "Softly and Tenderly," "How Great Thou Art," and "Rock of Ages." She remembers the lilies at Easter, the poinsettias and the tree covered with Chrismons during some magical days in December, and the Christmas play when some lucky child donned the freshly pressed white acolyte robe with a little halo to be the Christmas angel. In the summers, when it got pretty hot, lemonade and cookies would be served on the church lawn after worship, and people would have a chance to visit.

It was just kind of a very loving feel to it. It felt like you belonged somewhere. Really every Sunday was just comforting and just the right thing. It just felt right. [Penny]

Dan lived across town and went to a different church, an old country church with the cemetery right beside and a bell you rang with a rope. Like Penny, Dan's family was very involved in the church. There were the plays and dinners after church. His mom sang in the choir.

When he was 12 years old, Dan's oldest brother was killed in a car wreck.

I can see that day like it was yesterday: my dad coming to get me and my brother out of school, coming home, and my mom sitting there. I just knew something wasn't right. I didn't know what. As the week sort of unfolded I saw a lot of things. There was one minister who came, an associate minister at the big church. I remember him commenting, "Don't listen to this junk about people telling you your brother's in a better place and all that. You need to feel grief and you need to understand that he wasn't meant to die at this time. God doesn't create people to die when they're 19. You need to understand that about God. He didn't cause this to happen."

There were other people saying, "Oh, it was meant to be . . . ." It was kind of confusing for a 12-year-old.

I remember there was a guy who was an executive at this company that my father worked for out of Winston-Salem. I remember him sleeping on our couch for over a week. He never left and I thought that was kind of weird as a 12-year-old, but as I've gotten older, I thought he really gave of himself that week. A lot of people did. That was definitely a life-changing experience for me. I can pick up little pieces of what went on in that week that I still carry with me—things I saw, things I heard, things that helped me believe. I saw how my parents dealt with it. They certainly weren't alone and they knew they weren't alone. I saw people from the church taking care of us. These weren't just neighbors. I knew that man. I'd seen him at church. Bringing food, picking me up, and taking me somewhere I needed to go and stuff like that. I knew they were church people. And looking back, I know what they were doing. At the time it was just this nice man from the church coming to pick me up, or cooking, or whatever. But I know the connection now. [Dan]

Penny and Dan "just went" to church on Sunday. And when they got to that age, they "just went" to youth group. It was a huge a part of their lives, as much a given as eating meals or going to school. It was just what they did, and they try to make it that way for their children. The kids know when they get up on Sunday morning, they are going to church. There is no struggle, no pleas to sleep late. In fact, Caitlin looks forward to Sunday worship, where she regularly accompanies the hymns on her flute. Matthew likes to help his dad usher.

But faith is about more than Sunday mornings. Penny and Dan both strive to live their faith seven days a week, not just for a weekend hour or two. Penny reads the short devotionals in *The Upper Room*[7] and thinks about each selection for a day or so, trying to understand how it might speak to her life. She finds the reading helpful and is always glad when she makes the time to do it. She feels good about that aspect of her spiritual life. She is less satisfied with her prayer life.

I am really, really bad about going to church and then getting home and getting busy doing dumb, dumb stuff, to make a priority of laundry or whatever. I'll go a day and think, oh, I didn't pray today. But prayer is very important and I do notice on the days that I don't stop and pray, I don't feel like the day has gone as well. [Penny]

Dan does not do much reading, but he tends to find time to pray. He runs his own construction business with 20-some employees. The people who work for him know that the church is important and have often gone over to "fix whatever needs to be fixed." It is not like he and his co-workers "sit around and talk about John 3, but they know they can tell me stuff that's going on in their family." And Dan prays for them or sometimes shares their concerns with his men's Bible study at the church.

They think they work for a pretty neat company. We don't have fish on our cars or on our trucks or anything like that. I hope just by the way I present myself and do things, by the way I treat my employees and my customers that people can tell there's something different about me, other than my low IQ. You sort of hope by living your life, you're living out the gospel. [Dan]

That is probably exactly what the man who slept on Dan's living-room couch so many years ago (after the death of Dan's brother) was hoping.

Mission trips are one way Dan and Penny have found to live out the Gospel. Dan has gone once to Jamaica and three times to Mexico with St. Francis UMC. Penny has accompanied the church's youth group to Henderson Settlement in the Appalachian Mountains four times.

Dan's initial involvement was simple. He is a contractor and the church needed someone who knew how to build buildings. "If I have a gift, I have a gift to solve problems. I can understand how tab a and slot b go together. I am a civil engineer." So he joined the team, pleased to have found a tangible way to express his faith.

On his first trip to Mexico he was "pretty scared." After the team had been working together for a day or two, and Dan had been pushing everyone pretty hard, one of the church members had a talk with him. They went outside one night under a street lamp.

He grabbed me and said, "Look around you, son, do you see a Home Depot? Do you see a Lowe's? We're not in Charlotte. We're in Tequisquiapan, Mexico. Calm down. Take a deep breath. God sent you here and God's gonna get us through this. It's not you. You're a conduit." And he woke me up to the idea that you take your little piece of talent that you have and you share it with these people in Mexico. They have a whole lot more to give back. [Dan]

Years later, Dan still marvels at the welcome the team received from the local community. "We slept in their beds. They moved into their kitchens and slept on the floor while we slept in their beds."

His recent trip to Jamaica was probably his most intense, and definitely his most rewarding. The task was to take a 100-year-old church building with a rotten wood floor that was up off the ground three or four feet and put a concrete slab under it and fill in underneath with dirt. A team from St. Francis UMC designed the floor, corresponding 1,000 miles with faxes and e-mails and photos. More than 30 people went to Jamaica over the course of three weeks. In spite of their host's skepticism ("He kept telling us, 'You're crazy, you're crazy. It will take 16 weeks, it will take 16 weeks.'"), the project was completed on time. Kevin, the youth minister, brought along his guitar, and the kids sang. "I guess the international sign of love is the hymnal and a guitar."

Dan knows these mission trips can be life-changing experiences. How to make sure the lives stay changed is the question with which he continues to struggle.

You always come back on this mountaintop experience. The trick for you is to feel the same way six months after you get back to Charlotte, when you're sitting in that traffic, as you do today sitting here in Jamaica, feeling like you and God are one. Remember that when you get ready to cuss the guy in front of you because he's going too slow. You want to hold on to that mountaintop experience where you realize that these kids don't care what the Dow Jones Industrial Average is doing. They don't know what an IRA is. But they're as blessed as I am. They have nothing compared to what we count of as stuff, and yet they hug you and they love you and they sing songs with you. [Dan]

Each summer Penny goes with the youth up to the mountains in rural Kentucky to do repair work on people's homes, many of whom are out-of-work miners. Last year her team put siding on the roof of a young mother's trailer.

These people are really hard on their luck. They have so little, and they're so happy to have somebody come and do something to their house just to try to make it look a little bit better. I think the kids see that, and they feel real good about themselves. They all talk about how rewarding it is. What amazes them is that we are still in the United States. It's just a day drive, but it is nothing like where they live. It takes forever just to get to a Wal-Mart, and it's not even a big one. I think it helps the youth appreciate a little of what they have and take for granted. [Penny]

Penny is convinced that her own daughter, Caitlin, has been changed by the experience. She is more aware of how fortunate she is. The sense of family they encounter is very, very strong, and the kids see that even though the people whose homes they are working on do not have the things they have. . . .

Those people have what we're looking for. They have what we're trying to get, when you get right down to it, which is a connectional love. And they're happy, which is good for our kids to see. [Penny]

It makes an impact on 'em. It's kind of like, "eat your peas because there's starving children in China." You can't see the starving children in China, so it doesn't really connect. When they hear something about poverty or somebody doing without here, on the other side of Charlotte, I would dare say that those 10 or 12 kids have a vision of what that means and something you can do about it. Kevin never has trouble getting these kids to go to the Rescue Mission. Kids go. They go and, yeah, they have fun, and, yeah, they're with their friends and, yeah, they get to come home to their nice house, but they give up their two or three hours and they go down there; and I think they bring a little chunk back with 'em each time. It's a little piece; what they do with it is up to them. [Dan]

THE CHARLOTTE RESCUE MISSION

Sandy, Ben, Alex, and Hannah go home after church and have a sandwich. Then Ben takes Alex back to boarding school, Hannah goes to work on homework, and Sandy goes back to church.

There is a kitchen adjacent to the sanctuary. On Wednesday nights volunteers prepare a congregational dinner, which is served in the reconfigured sanctuary. The kitchen is not large, but it is certainly made to cook for crowds. Today Sandy is working on a meal for well over a hundred men. As part of its Lenten observance, St. Francis UMC is bringing dinner to the

Charlotte Rescue Mission, a transitional men's housing facility located in downtown Charlotte. She pokes through the refrigerator and finds a huge chicken potpie and lots of meatballs. There is garlic bread in the freezer.

Soon more people arrive and the mountains of food are organized. Some people have made salads, others lasagnas, others desserts, others "real rolls that had been set out to rise." The food is put in cars, and the caravan starts toward the Mission. Many people are unclear on the directions, so the group tries to stick together during the almost 30-minute trip into the center of town.

Lots of families join this adventure. Some bring young children. The kids have made place mats from colored construction paper, magic markers, and crayons (no doubt from Sandy's infamous office), which say things like "God loves you." The idea had been for the men to take the mats with them, but the little boy saying the blessing forgets to mention that, so they are left behind.

The church people set up the tables: place mat, fork, knife, spoon, drink, and then a plate filled with lasagna, salad, and bread at each place. There are piles of homemade desserts—brownies, pound cakes, chocolate marshmallow cakes, Rice Krispies bars—so many desserts that some of the scrumptious confections are left uncut to be eaten the next day. The kids, and some adults, are the waiters. Everyone keeps busy and easy conversation is as abundant as the baked goods. After the meal the kids take around big baskets filled with candy and ask the men if they would like some. At first most say they are full, "No, thank you." But after the third or fourth innocent inquiry, the men simply smile and help themselves, and the people, young and old, of St. Francis United Methodist Church continue their task of building church.

3

A Story to Tell: Concord Presbyterian Church, Delaware, Ohio

GINNY TEITT

Recalculating

$\mathcal{G}$inny Teitt was driving through the outskirts of Columbus. She had just picked up a weekend guest at the airport on the east side of town and now was headed toward Ohio State University Hospital on the west side. One of her parishioners was experiencing some serious complications following what was to have been a fairly routine surgical procedure, and Ginny wanted to pray with her. Before leaving the airport parking lot, Ginny set her global positioning system. Directions to the hospital appeared on the small glowing screen on her dashboard: "West on INTERNATIONAL GTWY toward SAW-YER RD, 1.9 miles. Merge onto I-670W toward COLUMBUS." Ginny began driving. Then she began talking.

She talked about megachurches, Willow Creek Community Church in South Barrington, Illinois, and Saddleback Church in Lake Forest, California. The newly consecrated Presbyterian congregation that she pastors does not aspire to be a megachurch. In fact, the 80 founding members of this fledgling ministry have agreed that once their congregation grows to 350 members, they will begin to think about planting another church. When they reach 500, they *will* plant another church. Being a part of a congregation that numbers in the thousands does not appeal to the parishioners of Concord Presbyterian Church. Still they cannot help but marvel at the successes of the megachurches in their area, like the Vineyard Church of Columbus and World Harvest Church, and wonder if there are lessons to be learned.

For example, Ginny asks out loud, "Where do all those members come from?" Concord Presbyterian may not aspire to numbers in the thousands, but they would be delighted if a few *hundred* more of God's faithful found their way to this freshly formed religious gathering. "Does a growing congregation tend to attract believers from other churches?" she continues. Some of the most active members at Concord are former Catholics. Others are Presbyterians who have chosen to transfer their memberships from nearby congregations. Or should a nascent congregation focus on reaching the unchurched, those looking for a faith community, often referred to as "seekers," as well as those yet to realize the need to make space for God in their lives?

Ginny is aware that these are multifaceted questions with multifaceted answers. Her church has had a hard time advertising. The church meets in a public elementary school and thus is not allowed to put a sign outside the building. But in any case the congregation has targeted the school community as a potential source of new members. Current members of the church have prepared lunch for the school staff as a way of getting acquainted. And they have volunteered to help parents refurbish the school's playground.

Another consideration is Concord's relationship with other churches in the area. Since Concord meets in a school, and the congregation's contract limits it to Sunday morning building use, the members have no place to do weddings, funerals, or special services (such as Good Friday or Christmas Eve). They have reached out within the Christian community, but, for a variety of reasons, no established congregations have stepped forward to welcome them. Ginny wonders if the church-planting method, where a small group from a well-established church moves out to form a new church while maintaining a connection to the original church, might not be an easier way to start out.

Ginny's probing, earnest inquiries were interrupted by a pleasant female voice. "Recalculating," the voice intoned. A new set of directions appeared on the dashboard's luminous screen.

"What about young people?" Ginny wondered. Concord's mission statement says the congregation is geared toward young people, ages 15 to 35. The question is, should the young people be allowed "to call the shots?" Who sets the agenda? Ginny shared that a few weeks ago some of the young people confronted her, "You think you know what we want, but what you really need to do is ask us." So the following Sunday after church, the congregation had a round-table discussion. Congregants began to hear different viewpoints and realized that things that bothered them were actually appealing to others. Silly Putty, stretched this way and that, is how Ginny describes herself, as she tries to chart a course and pastor the congregation. She knows she cannot please everyone. She has been trying to figure out how to please God.

"Recalculating," her automated companion interjected for a second time. Ginny noted the new directions and continued her ruminations.

Ginny is thinking about music—how to find a balance between contemporary and more traditional music in the worship service. Her church does not have an organ. They do not have a building. They worship in a school cafeteria. She mentions Saddleback again and how the pastors of that congregation believe the thread running through all successful worship is music. It is especially important to seekers. Music helps bring people closer to God. Ginny is intrigued by the realization that for hundreds of years the old hymns were simply talking about God and now contemporary Christian music is talking to God, personally. She believes the former may have provided a theological basis for understanding God, while the latter provides the passion for God. For her, the former without the latter is shallow, and the latter without the former is hollow. The original music minister at Concord "had the gift." His administrative skills were lacking (though she admitted hers are, too), but that young man was just amazing musically. He was able to bring people into the presence of God. Unfortunately he moved to Nashville.

"Recalculating," Ginny's guide interjected. Neither seemed troubled by the need for a third interruption or a fresh set of directions.

Another issue that concerns Ginny is gender. She is very conscious of her role as a woman pastor, a role that required considerable theological and sociological adjustment for her to accept. She talked about a 24-year-old woman, a single mother, who is living in Ginny's home. The Teitt family somehow knew the woman needed a place from connections in Maryland, where they used to live. The woman was being raised in the Mennonite Church, but she was not interested in being part of that religious community and so she had essentially been shunned. She had arranged to leave the community with a young man she met over the Internet, a plan no one was happy about, and so Ginny offered to take in the woman, and her four-month-old baby boy, as an alternative. In order to solidify the arrangements, Ginny met with some of the Mennonite Church leaders. She knew these men did not have much regard for her authority as a pastor. In fact, the young woman's father seemed to intimate that his daughter might be better off leaving in the middle of the night with the young man rather than living with a female pastor.

"Recalculating." Ginny glanced at the screen, registered the changes, turned the corner, and continued her story.

The conversation with these Mennonite men went on for some time and was quite emotional. They were touched by Ginny's concern, and finally they agreed to accept Ginny's offer of a temporary home for the woman and her son. As the meeting drew to a close, Ginny asked if they could pray before they dispersed. The men agreed and asked her to offer words to God, to lead the poignant, if somewhat pain-filled, supplication. She was startled, but grateful to be acknowledged by her colleagues.

Arriving at the hospital, Ginny turned into the 10th Avenue parking lot and visited with her parishioner. The situation was much better than expected. She got back into her car, got on the highway, and headed toward home.

Let it be known I never had any illusions about ministry; growing up as a PK [preacher's kid], and witnessing firsthand the demands and rigors, it was far from my mind that God would one day call me to this vocation.

These were the words that Ginny shared with those gathered at her service of installation at the Concord Presbyterian Fellowship. Yet ministry is in her blood.

My Grandpa Nash, who I met only through the memories of my mother, was an itinerant Methodist preacher, who led his family from Iowa farm communities to the Colorado eastern plains where he pastored small-town churches. He often fed his family from the gifts of his rural congregants that graced his front porch. Baskets from the garden harvest, live chickens in burlap bags were sometimes his pay. When the farmers explained that they would miss worship to get the melon harvest gathered, my grandfather showed up on Saturday in work clothes with my mother in tow to lend a helping hand so his flock could honor the Sabbath.

Ginny's parents were missionaries. They lived and served in remote African villages and later in New York City. The poverty and hunger that plagued so many of God's children allowed them little rest. Her father, Paris Reidhead, a conservative, evangelical pastor in the Christian and Missionary Alliance was guided by the mantra, "You're either a missionary or a mission field."

Paris Reidhead was a powerful, prophetic preacher. In 1964 he preached a sermon at a missionary training school that eventually led to the founding of the Bible Teaching Ministries, which provides pastors overseas with resources for sharing the Gospel message. Though his wife, Marjorie, worked tirelessly at his side—ministering to all those who crossed her path—Paris Reidhead never considered the ministry, and certainly not ordination, to be a woman's place. He made no secret of the hope he harbored until very late in life that one of his sons might take up the mantle of his ministry. These men, however, chose to devote themselves to different dreams; someone else would have to maintain Paris Reidhead's ministry.

Ginny was neither the eldest nor the youngest of the Reidheads' six children. Her love and her life were dedicated to her earthly father and her Heavenly Father, and it was she who was to continue her father's work. Yet she remained a product of her upbringing. Both father and daughter had some recalculating to do. In the hearing, and the telling, of the story of Ginny's one-and-a-half-year-old son's miraculous recovery after he had been given up for dead, Ginny and her father both realized they were being given a new set of directions.

On March 19, 1992, my father was dying and I was spending a lot of time with him. I was with my dad seven years, to the very hour, that Sam had laid in that pool. My dad knew the story, but he listened to me tell it again that day, and the whole thing hit him in another way. When my father heard the story this time, something happened. Until that moment I think my father thought he'd be healed from cancer. But then he said, "I'm gonna die. I will be leaving." And he told me a story about my grandmother, Ruby Perkins Reidhead. The year was 1919 and Ruby had given birth to her first child. The child was breach. The doctor came to the house and worked. The baby's neck was broken in the process. The doctor took the baby—his neck at a right angle and laid the baby aside. He came to my grandfather and said, "We've lost the baby, but we've saved the mother." My grandfather said, "No, it's not so. God has shown me that this baby is going to be a spokesperson for God." The doctor attended to Ruby and went to take care of the baby's body. The head had righted and the baby was breathing. My father said, "That was my birth." I had never heard that story. But I think my father realized there was something going on with God preserving lives. And then he said, "It's you. It's always been you. The call of God is on your life." So my story is that my father gave me the mantle of blessing and then died three days later.

Thus it was that his ministry became her ministry. Ginny was ready to accept, maybe even to welcome, this new direction. But there would be three more children and seven years before her recalculations led toward seminary and the ordained ministry. She entered Methodist Theological School in Ohio in 1997, a bold step for a stay-at-home mom, a 44-year-old mother of seven. Still, Ginny is the first to point out that there were women before her, "the courageous first wave of women pastors" who had already figured out the route. She was just following their path.

When Ginny arrived home, following her airport pickup and hospital visit, her daughter Rachel was almost finished cleaning. Every inch of the beautiful old farmhouse had been dusted, the bathrooms were shiny, and the kitchen was scrubbed. There was a little sweeping left to do and then the place would be ready. Rachel had come home from The Ohio State University to help prepare dinner for her brother Sam. Also a student at Ohio State, Sam was celebrating his 22nd birthday.

The afternoon was spent creating the feast for what was to be an amazingly happy family occasion. There may have been presents and there was a cake, but those things were almost unnecessary. The celebration was the sheer delight of this family and a few of their friends in being together. With very little pretense everyone talked some and laughed a lot, honestly enjoying each other's company. Six of Ginny's seven children were there (Sarah, the seventh, was in Australia, pursuing a master's degree in Peace and Conflict Resolution with a focus on Chinese Studies).

Though Ginny had been a full-time pastor for over three years, her role as mother and wife consumed her that evening. She cooked. She served; and she served some more. And when it was all over, she washed dishes. Her husband, Jim, ordinarily said the blessing before the family's meals, and tonight's dinner was no exception. The laughter was easily interrupted, and quiet settled over the cheery and contented flock. Holding the hands of those whom they cared for, more than any other in the world, the Teitt family (which in that family includes their friends) listened as Ginny's husband and Sarah's, Hannah's, Rachel's, Andrew's, Matt's, Justin's, and Sam's father thanked God for the food and for the blessing of Sam's life.

There was no reference to his miraculous start, to "his story"—the story that precipitated the most profound recalculation of Ginny Teitt's life, the story whose telling confirmed his daughter's call to the ordained ministry in the mind—and heart and soul—of Rev. Paris Reidhead. At 22 years, Sam is a healthy, hilarious young man. He told a few stories of his own that night, actually countless stories, of his amusing exploits, which left his family weeping with laughter. There were stories about food and football (after all, Sam attends Ohio State). There were reminiscences, like the time he was having a sleepover with his best friend, also named Sam, and one Sam got sick and threw up in the other Sam's face, literally. There were hunting stories—it was deer season and the men in the Teitt family are avid outdoor sportsmen. And there were practical joke stories, like the time someone wrote "a message" in the mud on his car, and he drove all around town and did not realize it was there until he got home. There was no shortage of Sam stories that evening, but even though it was his birthday, his birth story was not among the tales. Perhaps "the story" does not need to be told. Just as no reference was made to his gender or to his name, the story is simply part of Sam. Or perhaps, at this point in time, it is not really Sam's story, but rather his mother's response to "Sam's story" that warrants reflection.

[In the early 1980s] My husband's job took us to Memphis. While we were down there we had two boys and a girl. We took a risk in going down there. It was a great opportunity for my husband's career, but nothing panned out. He found a new job with the State of Maryland and moved back to the East Coast. I stayed to sell the house. It was a time of self-examination, of looking at our lives and saying, "Are we on the wrong path?" During that time I remember wanting to throw my Bible against the wall and tell God that I didn't like anything that was happening. I was a thousand miles away with three little kids. My husband was working on the East Coast. I couldn't sell the house. We didn't have a place to live. I picked up the Bible to throw it and instead hugged it to me. I remember kneeling. And I said, "I can't. I know you, God, and I trust you."

Finally we sold our house. And we bought a beautiful place on the eastern shore of Maryland, a five-acre little paradise. I was pregnant again and my husband kept waking up at night, dreaming there was something he needed to pray for. God was saying, "Wake up, you need to pray." And he'd say, "Okay, I'll pray, but I don't know what it is." Then he was woken up another night and it was something about oxygen deprivation. He realized it was his unborn child. He didn't tell me because I'd been through so much. Then Sam was born. He was blue-black because the umbilical cord was around his neck and there were two knots in it—two true knots and he was coding. They thought he was stillborn. The doctors syringed him out. They loosened the cord and they got him breathing. But they knew he had sustained an oxygen loss. They did an apcar reading and it was nine out of ten. Every reflex was normal. They thought he would be brain-dead. The delivering doctor had never seen a baby survive two knots in the umbilical cord. The little hospital called him the miracle baby. Jim picked up the baby and said, "Samuel, my son Samuel." And then he said, "Oh, I'm so sorry, you can name the baby. I didn't mean to name him." But we'd already talked about that name. We knew that it meant God had heard our prayers. That was Sam's birth.

So we had two boys, a girl, and then Sam. Samuel. He was always called Samuel until he got older; now he's called Sam. And I'm at a women's meeting at a little Methodist Church and the speaker shares about being willing to offer her life for God's purposes. She gave a really challenging talk. Will you give all that you have and honor to God for God's purposes? I was thinking, "God, will I really give you all that I have?" And I said, "Yes, I will give you all that I have." And I am driving home. It's a hot summer night. Sam had been in the nursery and now I had him in the car seat in the back. I came to a stop light. And I can still remember exactly where I was. I heard this other sense, "Oh, you'll give me everything—will you give me your children?" And it was asking, "Are you willing to give your child?" And I thought, "You can have anything, anything, my house, my car, not my children." And we drove a little further and I can picture Matthew, Justin, Sarah—Sam in the backseat—and I had this sense, "You can't hold onto something, if you think you can do better than I can." So I thought, "Okay, God, I give you my children. I give you my children and I am trusting you."

That was summer. The next spring, in March, I was at a prayer meeting. And while we were there my friend's little girl opened the door. . . . We had checked on them. They were all watching TV. . . . We checked on them again and two were missing. A door was opened. . . . We didn't know how it happened. When we found Sam, he was floating facedown in an ornamental fishpond. He was there for quite a while. I'd been a lifeguard and I remember my lifeguard instructor saying, "If you ever pull out a drowning victim, you better hope they're under the water, because if they're facedown on the surface you're pulling a corpse." And there he was unquestionably facedown floating on the surface. And I just remember saying, "No. In the name of Jesus, no." And I pulled him out—stone-cold and blue-gray. I knew I should breathe into him. He was all full of water; his lungs were full of water. But I remember thinking, "Well even if he's dead, Lazarus was dead for three days. If you were able to raise him, then I think you're able to raise Sam, but I don't know if you will." I went back to the house to call 911. I had given the baby to one of the other women. I don't know why I gave him to her. I went back to the house, and I fell on my face right inside the door and said, "God, I gave him to you; if this is why they called him a miracle at his birth, for 16 months of life, then you better help me, because I can't bear this. I can't bear it." And all of a sudden the words came to me that the Father should be glorified. And I knew Sam would live.

They tried everything they knew; Sam didn't respond. They got him to the hospital, called Code Blue. They worked and worked and worked—nothing. God had said Sam was going to live. The pediatrician came to fill out the death certificate, and Sam's finger went like that, which all the doctors knew was a muscle contraction, but the pediatrician said, "Don't stop." There were seven doctors working on him for over an hour. They were angry that his pediatrician wouldn't sign off, but they kept working and Sam came back.

But with that much oxygen deprivation, was he brain-dead? They flew Sam in a helicopter to Johns Hopkins. His pH was incompatible with life. The tests showed the early stages of decomposition. The doctors at Hopkins met the plane with a body bag. When we got there, I told them what happened, and they said, "That's what we heard. But we did a brain scan, and it was normal." On the third day we came in—we had been thinking we'd seen the resurrection—and they said, "He's not going to make it. His lungs have soaked up so much water and the bacteria are taking over. We're loosing his organs one by one. He's not going to make it another hour."

Jim and I went down to the chapel at Johns Hopkins. We were depleted, just depleted and were at the chapel praying, just praying. The chapel door opened and a woman came in dressed in a nice black suit, but carrying a rumpled paper grocery bag, such an odd combination. She went up to the altar, pulled a big, huge, coffee-table Bible out of her rumpled bag. She opened it on the altar, knelt in front of it, and began to pray out loud. Now, a friend in Memphis had called and said, "God keeps giving me this Psalm." And she [the lady in the suit] started reading that Psalm (Psalm 46). The last thing she said was, "Be still and know that I am God." And this vision came to me. I saw Jesus welcoming the little children, the lambs, the Jesus of the Bible pictures holding Sam, just holding him. And Jesus said, "Sam, it has been a precious time, but it's not time." And in my mind's picture Jesus put him down on his little toddler feet and pushed his bottom and in my mind's picture my husband's hands were reaching and he said, "It's time to go back." And Jim welcomed him. At the same time the doctors are telling us Sam's not going to live.

The woman in the nice black suit sang, not in our language. She began to sing this song that was the most haunting, beautiful song you could ever think of. Then she disappeared and we never saw her again. We went back up, and this young, crackerjack pathology doctor who would not give up trying to find out what kind of bacteria was in Sam's body discovered it was an anaerobic bacteria which lives in the absence of oxygen. It required a very specific antibiotic. They gave it to him and the infection receded.

Well, the little lady who had told us where the chapel was had a seven-year-old grandson who had been hit by a pickup truck, crossing a pretty big highway. He was in the most extreme coma, traction, et cetera. She came every day and prayed for him. The neurologist had told them, "The boy is not just brain damaged. It's gone. Half the contents of his brain are gone. He'll never speak. He'll never move his right side. He'll never do this; he'll never do that." The mother came up to me and said, "I heard what the doctors said about Sam. All you had to do is just walk into the room [to help Sam], and now we need you to be near Frankie." This was hard. It was hard for me to hear that, because what hope they had built up by looking at Sam. If God could do that for Sam, why couldn't He do that for Frankie? They took us to Frankie. And they said, "We have no idea how long he'll be in the hospital, if he'll ever be able to breathe on his own." And we were like...but then you realize God had us here for other purposes. So I walked up to Frankie, and I held him and touched him on his arm. It felt like Gumby. It felt like clay or something because he was in that absolute coma. I held him and said, "God, if you created him in the first place, you could recreate what's gone. You've done so much for our son." Right then Frankie lifted his right arm off the bed. And they said he'd never move the right side of his body. And I was like, "God, you're going to have to pick me right up off the floor if this keeps going on."

Two weeks to the day from when Sam went into the hospital, they came in and said, "We took an x-ray, there's not even scar tissue. It's a perfect x-ray, there is nothing wrong. You can go home." We stopped at our pediatrician's office on the way home, and he grabbed Sam from me. Now this is a guy who has the bedside manner of a stump. And he goes running out the door into the hospital, into the pathology lab, into the emergency room. And he's saying, "It can't be. Look at him, look at him. It's a miracle." Later I'm in the grocery store with Sam, and I look over and there's a picture of Sam in the newspaper. The headline says, "Toddler who cheated death comes home. See Dead Toddler." The Associated Press picked it up. And people wanted me to tell the story.

Numerous churches invited Ginny to tell the story—even those churches that traditionally prohibit women from preaching. Women were allowed to share testimony, so she testified. She began to experience the power of the spoken word, the power of her spoken word. At the same time Ginny was leading a study on women and the Bible for her local church. Her preparation far exceeded the demands of the study. Rightly so since, although she did not realize it at the time, she was preparing for much more than a weekly Bible class. She sat at the kitchen table with biblical commentaries piled around her. She read everything she could find.

I was like Frederick Douglass. He was taught in his church that blacks had to serve whites. Then he had this epiphany. He said, "I'm not who you say I am." I went straight to the Greek, the original, and I said, "This is not true. This is not at all true. Women can serve God in any way. I can serve God in any way."

Still the notion of entering the ministry had not quite occurred to her. During this time, her time of epiphany, Ginny was having lunch with a friend, the woman whose little girl had opened the door on that fateful day. Her friend looked her straight in the eye and said, "You are meant to go to seminary. God is calling you to ministry." Ginny knew it was the truth, but she was not sure what to do about it.

Then she began waking up in the middle of the night with the feeling that God was telling her there was someplace she needed to go. She was a homemaker and she had a lovely home. Her husband had a good job. Jim was content in Maryland. He did not like change. He was the guy whose mother still lived in the house where he grew up, and Jim liked it that way. And yet she heard herself telling her husband, "We have to move." Jim did not feel what Ginny was feeling. This time he was not the one being awakened in the middle of the night with the urge to pray. But he could see how strongly Ginny was being called, so he agreed to look for another job. They would go wherever it was God was sending them.

Ginny felt a little like the prophet Abraham, asking her family to prepare for a journey whose destination was not yet clear. "Okay, pack up the van; I'll tell you when we get there." It turned out Jim's company was looking for someone to manage its Midwest office. So the Teitt's, all nine of them, moved to Columbus. At the time Ginny had no idea that Methodist Theological School in Ohio was only 20 minutes away from her new home.

Although she had instigated the move, Ginny had a "rough time" making the transition to life in Ohio. She was conflicted about her own identity—her purpose, her place. All of her kids were now in school. She knew she had to do something. Sort of casting about she decided to study for the law school admission tests. She also took a church history course at the Methodist Theological School in Ohio. The professor of that course, a woman with whom Ginny felt an immediate connection, was assigned as her advisor. Ginny took another course, and she realized "it was working okay." So she enrolled full time, or at least she tried to. Ginny filled out all the paperwork for the Masters of Theology program and met with her esteemed advisor, now mentor, to secure the requisite signatures. Her advisor refused to sign.

"You're in the wrong major. Move to pastoral ministry; that's what you're called for. It's so clear. Your gifts are so clear. Change your major; you're not a master of theology. You're called into ministry. Everything about you says that." She was right, so I did. It took me four years [to complete my degree]. My family got in the way. I had five kids at the house. Four of ours and one that we'd taken in, a girl whose mother died and her father took her on the weekends. I remember getting them ready, packing all the lunches, dropping them at a friend's house to catch the school bus to get to my 8:30 A.M. classes.

Ginny was certainly not the only woman in the class of 2001, nor was she the only second-career student. However, most of her academic associates were leaving careers as doctors or lawyers, bankers or business people. They were not quite sure what to make of this vibrant, almost middle-aged, woman who spoke unapologetically about her very concrete experiences of God's power in her life, and *her* career—which spanned more than two decades and had produced seven wonderful children—as a full-time mother.

The first class entered Methodist Theological School in Ohio in 1960 in the midst of the tumult of the Vietnam War and civil rights struggles. The institution proudly nurtures its reputation as a leader in progressive theological studies. Ginny Teitt had been raised as a conservative evangelical. Her desire to share her heart for God, lived out in a conservative evangelical faith as a trained professional, led her to seminary. Seminary was challenging. She was challenged politically. She was challenged socially. And she was challenged theologically.

I was put in this world where I really had to rethink. If there was ever a liberation theologian, it was my father. But liberation theology comes out of the other side politically. So I'm in this setting with people who are all really focused and very, very anti anyone who isn't labeled what they're labeled. And I realize that the label that my dad would have had is evangelical, conservative, and Republican. And I am studying where they label themselves totally the opposite. But I am thinking, "He loved God. He totally loved God." The students here are committed to causes which are good, and I love them. I love these people. I know they had radical, real encounters with God. But it's so polarized. I have to hide where I come from because it feels like they would hate me if I told them where I come from. But my dad was like these people. He was radical. He was on the front line, daring and challenging. Polarization is the power of darkness. We can't dialogue with each other. I can't label myself; I don't know how someone else can label me.

With a few years' hindsight and countless more encounters with people of faith, Ginny welcomes the questions, the indecision. It is the people who have it all figured out that "scare" her more than anything. "I don't care what side you're on, if you think you have it all figured out, that scares me."

Jesus tells us there are those who "have ears to hear" and there are some that simply will not hear. Perhaps some of us are called to be ear healers.

Ginny does not have deep Presbyterian roots. At the time she was in seminary, her family was attending a Presbyterian church. As she neared the end of her studies, her decision to seek ordination in the Presbyterian Church was practical as well as theological. The Presbyterian's call system suited her much better than, for example, the appointment system of The United Methodist Church.[1] The former gave Ginny, and her family, the opportunity to have more input into where she would minister. At the time of her ordination, her two youngest children were still in high school, and most of the others had settled in the Columbus area. She had no interest in moving. Ginny called the presbyter and inquired if there were any local positions available. He told her the area had been targeted for new church development. Even before she finished her student internship, she convened a meeting with 18 people to organize a new Presbyterian Church.

It was early April of 2003 when the seed dream first was planted for this Delaware County Presbyterian New Church Development. For nearly one full day I danced with excitement about the possibilities, until in the dark the next night I awoke with the weight of the reality of what all that meant. "Not me, I don't think so. . . ." And then I heard the familiar voice of God speaking to my heart, "If you think you can do it, that is reason to fear; but if you know that I can do anything through you, then put your trust in me." Truthfully there have been many times since those first 18 people attended an informational gathering that I asked God, "Just what were you thinking?"

Fifty-two people came to worship on Pentecost Sunday, June 8, 2003, at the Acres Party House, fondly remembered as the "first Pentecost party house premier." About 35 of those were committed to creating a new church. Others had come to "see us off." A little over two years later, Concord Presbyterian Church has been consecrated by the presbyter and has close to 150 worshippers at its weekly services.

A number of factors aided the church's development, not the least of which was Ginny's family. Five of her children are deeply involved in the ministry. They invited their friends. Their friends invited their friends, and "instant youth group." Then their friends got their parents to come.

Some of the greatest stories that we have of lives changed are parents that came because their kids were finding something. It's not a clever strategy or campaign. It's being in the right place at the right time.

To those at Concord, the right time is God's time.

We have learned that spiritual power is contingent on communion with God. If there is one key I can identify that may assure our success, it is that we have been saturated in prayer.

Commitment to mission has also been pivotal. The first committee to be formed in the church was the missions committee. A significant portion of the budget has been allocated for missions, which has been a challenge for some of the more business-minded church leaders. But as long as Rev. Ginny Teitt is their pastor, Concord will not cut back on missions spending. She believes the church is not only called to mission, that is why the church exists. She is not troubled that she is counseling her congregation to give away money when it does not have enough.

Though plans for their own building are only in the most formative stage, she is preparing her congregation to do mission work in Ethiopia, to help build schools, and perhaps someday medical facilities. Four members of the congregation, including Ginny, went to Ethiopia on what they called a "visioning trip" to nurture a partnership with a remote village struggling to overcome poverty and illiteracy. The call Ginny feels compelled to answer is feeding the hungry, comforting the sick, and housing the homeless.

I minister to a very diverse group of people from across the social, political, and religious spectrum. I see a hunger to serve God and to live beyond their own agendas, from all of the camps. I don't agree with anyone, including my own self, all of the time. I see lives transformed by vibrant encounters with God.

I think we are in grave need of political reform. Campaigns are bought. We are a country and maybe a world that is dictated by money, which may be the root of evil. This corruption knows no national or political boundaries. This corruption is changed in an individual from the inside out. My faith compels me to pray and fast (I have been fasting—water only one day a week) for the leadership of this nation, the needs of the world, and the ministry with which I have been entrusted.

Ginny readily identifies "political, social, moral, and economic actions that regard only self and self-promotion and satiation of personal appetites with no consideration or regard for the cost or consequences to anyone other than corporate or individual self" as sin. Yet, haggling about the systemic causes of poverty or the thorny social and political issues confronting the church does not interest her.

If we can just work alongside each other feeding the hungry, doing the things we can all agree that the Bible tells us to do, then the other stuff will follow. When people honestly and truly encounter God, they change. They move from seeking to employ God's benefits in their own lives to participation in the work of God for the redemption of the world. When the rich young ruler sought salvation he asked, "What must I do to be saved?" Jesus told him to sell his possessions, not to earn his salvation, but to discover and experience it.

Ginny is content to move on with faith and trust God for the resources (read finances). Though she laughs and admits that a congregation that focuses on young adults and teenagers may find it difficult to build a solid financial base since even if she were to convince the young people to tithe, their gifts would total about $12 a week. Still this humble yet prophetic woman who pastors "the church where women preach and men cry" remains ready and willing to allow God to be her guide.

I would rather close down being faithful to the vision than not be faithful to the vision in order to protect finances. If the church doesn't make it and we've been faithful to the vision, that must be God's will. I believe that God will provide. I walk by faith. I always have.

PAM STOCKDALE

Her Father's Daughter

I remember the first time she got up in our church and told the story about Sam, I didn't like her. I didn't like her at all. I didn't like that story. There wasn't a dry eye in the place except me. It actually just pissed me off. I was having problems sleeping at the time, bad problems—couldn't sleep, couldn't sleep. And it made me mad 'cause I thought, "Her faith is so strong. She has such a close relationship with God that her child can come back from the dead. My faith isn't even strong enough that I believe I can sleep at night."

Pam Stockdale is a happily married businesswoman. She is a leader in her church and is just finishing construction on a lovely home with lots of glass to afford generous views of her "little bit of woods." By all accounts she is a successful Christian woman. Although there have been times in her life when the Christian part has not come easily, these days she finds strength and comfort in her faith and openly shares that faith with others, especially on the job. Pam is a national graphics sales representative for the Packaging Corporation of America.

She knows that it is "not politically correct" to talk about God, but anytime the door is opened, she steps through. Co-workers have shared their grief with her at times of death. They have approached her with big questions about the meaning of life. A few months ago, a new hire called her. He told Pam that he had prayed God would put at least one Christian in his path at work. Pam talked with him for a long time. Before they hung up, he asked her to pray with him. Another colleague overheard Pam talking about her faith. He was young and encountering a few too many distractions in his life. He was having a hard time honoring his faith and welcomed the opportunity to speak with her.

For years she had been the butt of the jokes in the salesroom because she was the only woman. She had made peace with that. So risking the effects of unapologetically revealing her religious commitments was not that bold a step. She recalls a regional company meeting where each salesperson was asked to share one thing they used to get them in the door. Many of Pam's stories centered around Bible study or other church gatherings. As she concluded her talk she added that she did everything she could, then she put it in God's hands. Some colleagues sat in the back of the room and laughed at what they perceived to be a woman's naiveté. But afterwards others praised her courage for talking honestly in religious terms. Pam has allowed herself to become vulnerable in her workplace, and she feels okay about that.

In her personal life, in her professional life, and even in her politics, Pam is convinced of the power of prayer and faithful witness. One's religion is not something to be sequestered, taken out only in times of crisis or in the most solitary moments. On the contrary, one's faith is a part of every conversation, every action regardless of who you are or to whom you are talking.

I love having a president in the White House that prays. George Bush is not a good speaker; I mean he's a horrible public speaker. He embarrasses one. "Oh, please be quiet and get that stupid grin off your face, because it looks so idiotic." And then you turn around and I think about 9/11 and how he handled that, and I shudder when I think that could have been Al Gore. That would have been disastrous.

I like the fact that there's a president in the White House that is not afraid to let his faith be known. I don't agree with everything George Bush has done, but I do believe he is genuine about his faith. It shows in a lot of his actions. I know some people that have had one-on-one encounters with him when the world wasn't watching, and their stories have deepened my respect for him.

Pam believes the government's attentions should be focused on issues such as religious freedom, support for the family, child abuse, defense, and health care. Consistency and character are what she looks for in a candidate. She appreciates having people of faith in positions of political leadership.

I hope a person of faith would be more other-centered and realize that there is someone greater than him- or herself in control. Just as a child wants to do the right thing out of love for a parent, a person of faith desires to please God out of love and gratitude for Him. And that includes making decisions based on truth and love as opposed to greed and power and a strong sense of accountability to the welfare of those they serve. But I don't think you can dictate morality. You can't govern it.

Pam has some questions about the influence of the Christian Right on American politics. She finds the term itself is cause for concern.

I don't like the generalization "Christian Right" because it has a bad connotation. I AM the Christian Right. I am a Christian and I am conservative in my political beliefs. But I don't want to hear politics coming from the pulpit, and I don't want politics using Christianity to enforce certain religious beliefs on "we, the people."

Pam's commitment to family and her respect and appreciation for authority emerge from the context of her own loving and supportive family. She had an "idyllic childhood," kind of like the Cleavers, the all-American family featured in the 1950s television show *Leave It to Beaver*.

I never appreciated it or understood how incredible that was until I got older and started talking to other people—I thought everybody lived that way.

She grew up in a Christian home. Her family said grace at dinner. And although she does not remember her parents talking much about religion, she never doubted that they shared a strong faith. They went to church every Sunday. She went to Sunday School and was in the annual church pageant. The church played a vital role during Pam's adolescent years.

When I was in seventh grade, the youth group in the church was called Cairo. Everybody went to youth group because it was the only way you could get out of the house on Sunday nights. You weren't allowed to go out and do anything else. At youth group you got to be with boys. I went to church camp in the summers. That's where I learned how to shoot craps and play cards and all that kind of stuff.

Like Pam, her father was in sales.

He was always happy, always up. He treated everybody the same. It didn't matter if you were the president or the janitor. He told me I could do anything I wanted to. It never dawned on me that being a woman could be an issue in the workplace. The other thing he told me was as long as you can look yourself in your eye and talk to God and feel comfortable with what you've done, it's okay.

Pam's dad had an accident when she was six years old. He was thrown out of a car and into a telephone pole on Christmas Eve. He was in the hospital a long time. Six years later, her father was hit by a car again. It was in the same week that President John F. Kennedy was assassinated. Her father was walking across the driveway of a parking garage, and a woman came speeding out of the garage and hit him, knocking him across the street onto a parked car. The hood ornament went through his leg and pinned him there. The woman never took her foot off the accelerator, so she just kept hitting him. The police came to Pam's home and reported her father's death. The accident was announced on the radio. When Pam's grandmother heard that her son had died, she had a heart attack.

But when the rescue team got him to the hospital, they got his heart going again. Another long hospital stay ensued. Gangrene set in and his leg had to be amputated. The surgery was risky at best. Fearing the worst, Pam waited with her family. Finally a nurse came out and told those assembled that her father, Robert Lee Deer, had died during surgery. The grieving family left the hospital. Sometime later, when the orderlies were wheeling him down to the morgue, her father's arm fell off the gurney. The person who reached down to resettle the dead man's arm felt a pulse.

Robert Deer's recovery was amazing, emotionally and spiritually, as well as physically. He was in the hospital for almost a year. He helped other patients who had lost limbs deal with their unwitting sacrifice. He organized wheelchair races in the halls. Robert Deer and his mother were practical jokers. Pam remembers the time his mom helped her adult son wrap rubber maggots in his bandages in anticipation of the surgeon's visit to check the progress of his wound.

He would do stuff like that all the time. He just had an incredible sense of humor through the whole thing. We talked about that years later when he got cancer. We were having lunch one day and I said, "Are you scared about dying?" And he said, "No, I've done that before." He asked if I was scared and I said, "I am petrified. I just can't imagine life without you. I can't imagine not having you here to call to ask for advice. Or just to have your love." He said, "Is that something I gave you?" And I said, "Yeah." He said, "Well, that's not going to go away."

I know he had a very strong faith, but he wasn't one of those....you know he lived it. He was an insurance salesman. He loved people. He loved to take scripture out of context. I remember a speech he made one time, "Let me not hear the tinkling of coins, but the soothing rustle of bills...."

Pam was close to her father whom she remembers fondly as "her soul mate." And her stepfather—her mother remarried after her father's death—was "like a carbon copy of my father, just lovely, so sweet." For many of her friends their faith journey includes sorting through a troubled father-daughter relationship. Having faith in God, the Father, is problematic since many of Pam's friends do not want to have anything to do with a God that even vaguely resembles their earthly fathers. Pam had two loving fathers.

I can remember reading the verses about how much a father loves his children and how much more does your Heavenly Father love you...that would be like wow!

Without a doubt Pam had a solid foundation for her faith, but there have been moments in her life when she still needed a bit of shoring up. A few years ago, her husband, Chip, was diagnosed with cancer. Pam had lost her father and her mother to the dreaded disease. Chip's prognosis was not good, and Pam was not sure she could handle the situation. A woman from the church, an oncology nurse, stepped in. She got Chip to an excellent doctor the next day. Chip would be operated on the following Monday.

At church that Sunday, the whole congregation laid hands on Chip to pray for him. Chip arrived at the hospital on Monday morning confident, not the least bit frightened. Pam took comfort knowing that everybody else was praying for her husband, because she simply could not. Church members waited with her on the day of the surgery. "It was like a mob." An hour and a half into the surgery (which the doctors had warned her could last as many as ten) the doctor came out and said the operation was over. After the lab reports came back, they sent Chip up to recovery. An hour later he was in his room.

I know it was a miracle, and you'll never convince him that it wasn't. He went for his follow-up and he said, "What was it?" And the doctor said, "I don't know." Chip turned his life around 360. Now he's always working at the church, going to Bible studies, et cetera.

Pam acknowledges the weak moments in her faith, when she drew strength from her father or the other members of her church, those who prayed for her husband when she could not find the way. She tells her father's story and she tells Chip's story, each in their own way miraculous. But she has a story of her own, one which many, who have found themselves in similar situations, hear and immediately recognize the presence of the Divine.

Chip is Pam's second husband and she is his second wife. Chip has a son named Kevin from his previous marriage. Initially after his father remarried, Kevin was with his father every other weekend and on Wednesdays. Chip's ex-wife got along well with Pam. In order to normalize everyone's lives, Chip and Pam bought a house closer to Kevin's mom so Kevin could divide his time equally between the two houses and easily attend the same school. The three adults shared the responsibility for raising Kevin. They consulted on everything. They did not always agree, but they found ways to determine what was best for him. For his part Kevin embraced Pam. On Mother's Day he made two Mother's Day presents.

Then when Kevin was in the seventh grade, his mom resigned from her job and decided to be a full-time mom. Pam was angry. She had helped raise Kevin for so many years; she did not want to give him up. She told Kevin she would still pick him up and bring him to church—their weekly mother-son ritual. Now Kevin wanted to bring his mom. He thought she needed a church. Pam resisted. Church was the one place she went with Kevin where she was not "the stepmother." She wanted to guard this space, to protect her own little sanctuary. But Kevin persisted and Pam heard God agreeing with Kevin, telling her to call Kevin's mother and invite her to church. God's message was clear, yet Pam refused. Again and again God made His will known to her. Again and again, Pam said no, until she just couldn't anymore.

Finally I said, "Okay, God. I will do this, but you will have to change my heart."

So Pam made the call. And the two women took Kevin to church. They dropped Kevin off at his Sunday School class and Kevin's mother accompanied Pam to the adult class.

People said, "Oh, is this your sister?" "No, it's Kevin's real mom, Chip's ex-wife." It was horrible.

Over time the women shared childhood stories, dreams, and aspirations. They both became heavily involved in the church and once even shared a room on a retreat. Their relationship became a ministry of sorts as they encountered other divorced people in hurting relationships.

I'm not going to say it was always easy. It wasn't. At times I got really jealous. At times I was really hurt. But there were so many people who just couldn't believe it was possible, and I said, "Well, without God, it wouldn't be possible."

Pam Stockdale is, without a doubt, her Father's daughter.

Ginny pulled the laundry basket out of the closet. It was filled with carefully folded, colorful linens and handmade quilts. Before putting it in her car she put a few big bags of broccoli and a very sweet-smelling pecan pie on top. In what seemed like an afterthought, she grabbed the wooden bowl of gourds from the middle of her dining-room table, and then a couple of candles. When everything was in the car, Ginny's words of explanation were simply, "creating sanctuary."

The next stop was "the house" or, for the uninitiated, the offices of Concord Presbyterian Church located in a split-level residence not far from the elementary school where the young congregation holds its Sunday services. Ginny went into the house and returned, gingerly carrying a medium-size table that she added to her backseat, "the altar." It is Sunday morning and in addition to interpreting the word of God to her congregation, Ginny also feels called to create a sacred space, a sanctuary of sorts, for the faithful.

Though one would be hard-pressed to find a typical Sunday at Concord, today has been set aside for something special. After church the congregation will join in its first Harvest Lunch. With Thanksgiving on the horizon, the idea was to set aside some time to celebrate with the church family, since most people would be away on the holiday itself. The deacons are in charge, and someone offered to bring a deep-fried turkey. The people of Concord like to spend time together. They like to just sit around talking about everything, from football to term papers to sweet potatoes to conversing with the canonized.

TONY EYERMAN

Something Else Out There

We never considered ourselves Roman Catholics. We considered ourselves American Catholics, which is different. And if being a Presbyterian means you have to give up the saints and give up Mary, then we're really not Presbyterian either. The other day at church a woman asked my wife, Patti, "Do you worship Mary and the saints?" And Patti said, "No, not really." By way of explanation, she looked at the woman and said, "I don't know your husband very well, but could you do me a favor and see if you could get him to do this and this and this? It's like this is God and this is Mary and there are times I just can't talk to Him, and so I've got to ask Mary to speak to Him." We're not asking Mary to save us. All we're asking for is to have Mary and the saints put in a good word for us.

...just repeating the Hail Mary again and again and again puts my soul at rest. It's just a comfortable state. It has nothing to do with me worshiping Mary. It's just having her to lean on puts me in a better presence of God. If someone needed to get my attention and they couldn't, there's one person that can, other than my wife, and that's my mother. And I can hear my mother saying, "John Anthony..." And I can hear Mary saying, "Jesus...." That's how Mary is in our lives. I can imagine this mother, telling her son, "Tony needs help now."

John Anthony Eyerman was born and raised a Catholic. His grandfather was one of 12. His grandmother was one of 8. His grandfather was German. His grandmother was Irish. Though acknowledging the "merger," he still describes his as a "good, traditional Irish-Catholic family." Tony's father is also one of 12. His extended family, centered around the north end of Columbus, is very large, very tight, and very Catholic. He references the movie *Avalon,* a kind of lost Americana, by way of explanation. Two of his uncles attended seminary, but left school before becoming priests.

Tony is the oldest of three. He went to Catholic elementary school and Catholic high school. His family attended mass every Sunday. They occupied "the same spot in the same pew, every nine o'clock mass." Tony's dad was a lector and Tony was an altar boy. During high school (1972–1976) he was exposed to the Brown Franciscan nuns out of Lewiston, New York. They were a bit more liberal than the Dominican nuns from Columbus that Tony was used to. In fact, his encounter with the Brown Franciscans was the first time Tony saw a nun wearing something other than a habit.

Vatican II, Pope John XXIII, the civil rights movement, and the Vietnam War ("I was old enough to remember, but young enough to miss it.") are the scenes that form the backdrop for Tony's religious formation. He was guileless. And his munificent spirit enabled him to nurture tolerance along with a deep faith commitment.

Tony met his wife, Patti, at a Catholic retreat. She had come to Ohio from Buffalo, New York, to attend Ohio State, where Tony was starting his junior year. The rest is "Catholic retreat history." They were married a little over a year later at the Newman Center run by a Paulist Order, "which is about as liberal a Catholic as you can be." All three of their children were baptized at the Newman Center. But eventually the couple graduated from Ohio State. A move to Charleston, South Carolina, forced them to leave behind their comfortable, somewhat counterculture, college Catholicism.

Charleston, South Carolina is still considered a missionary state by the Catholic Church. There were one or two [Catholic] churches in all of Charleston. I think there are only four or five in the whole state.[2] So we kind of took quite a leap back with a very traditional church. We were just making ends meet and my oldest daughter was two. We had another one born down there. It was just too far from home, and we moved back after a couple of years. Since then we've been kind of homebodies, staying in the central-Ohio area.

Upon their return, Tony and Patti found a church in Marysville, exactly what they had hoped for—lots of young families, like theirs. One of the priests was a friend from "the retreat days." There was a lot of support for their family and a lot of work out in the community. The Eyerman's were actively involved in that parish for seven years, but after about five years, the diocese changed their priest. Their progressive friend was moved out and an older, more conventional priest moved in.

This guy came in and he was real traditional—men are men and women are women. And by then I had three daughters and a very equal, very loving wife. He proceeded to tell my wife where she belonged in the hierarchy of the family and the hierarchy of the church. He said a couple of things he shouldn't have. We decided to just bow out gracefully rather than make a big to-do.

Tony and his family found another church in the area, but somehow the energy was not quite right—theologically or socially. Tony was looking for social awareness, not a social life. He wanted a place that would enable his family to do the work of the Lord outside the walls of the church, not just find a sanctuary to pontificate about it within.

One day Ginny Teitt asked Emily, Tony's youngest daughter, then 18, if she would come and play keyboards at Ginny's new church. The Eyerman's had known the Teitts for a long time. Each of Tony's three daughters had been in the same grade as one of Ginny's kids. But they had known each other without really knowing each other. As Tony put it, "They were busy with their kids, and we were busy with ours. We'd pass each other in the halls in school on teacher-parent night, say 'hello,' be social; but that was it." Without any significant parental consultation, Emily accepted Ginny's invitation and began playing keyboards at Concord Presbyterian Fellowship. Her parents had learned that if they pushed too hard, their girls, now young women, would rebel. The wise parents decided to "just go along" with Emily, figuratively and literally. Tony and Patti attended a service.

We were afraid that God was going to cast us out into the wilderness if we left the Catholic Church. We'd been going for generations.

It was after a spirit-filled Christmas Eve service that the protective yet honest parents admitted that they were no longer just "checking on Emily." They were finding something for themselves.

We thought, "You know what? There's something else out there." We'd been looking. We'd always considered going somewhere else and just.... It wasn't fear, but maybe uneasiness or I don't know what it was. But it's approaching a year since we started actively becoming involved in Concord. And I guess now we're Presbyterians. We actually changed our membership.

Tony is clear that getting to Concord was the easy part. Emily was playing, her parents wanted to support their daughter, share in her success. The venue was incidental. They were going to hear Emily's music. They were churchgoers. Sure they were Catholic, but it did not occur to them that they would feel uncomfortable in this worship setting. But neither did it occur to them that they would feel so comfortable. Somehow Ginny managed to extend her mother's love, her family to the entire congregation. Tony and Patti began to witness and to feel the loving family spirit moving through the entire congregation. They were made welcome. And the stories began to flow. Now Tony finds himself telling the story of Concord.

We're a God-based, faith-based community. We accept you as you are, no matter who you are or where you are, what story you have to tell. Some of you have a great story, some of you have awful stories—we're all still here.

Tony found himself repeating the phrase "Catholics don't have a lock on heaven" with a new sense of commitment and understanding. He had a long talk with Ginny during which they agreed that what matters in the end is how you treat your brothers and sisters; God would probably not ask "new arrivals" if they were Catholic or Protestant.

These were not new ideas for Tony; he had always been comfortable with other faiths. But never had his openness been tested in such a concrete manner. It had been much easier to be open to other paths when he was securely ensconced in the comfort of his own.

Shortly after I got out of college, I was approached by my boss. And he started in on me about needing to convert to his church. And I told the guy, "Look, this is a road map. To get here from Montana there are about a thousand different ways to go. But we'll all get there. I might take a different route, but we'll get there all the same. That's how I envision our faith journey. We're all going to get there, hopefully. Some people might take a wrong turn and never turn around and come back. There are a lot of different ways to get there, but we'll all get there. I've chosen this route." And from that point on he left me alone.

Tony seemed startled not by the confirmation of his belief that different routes existed, but by the fact that *he* was altering *his* course. But the intimate Christian family he found at Concord captivated him. He recalls the story of a good friend who also grew up Catholic. After his friend's divorce the Catholic Church refused to bless his second marriage. His friend left the Catholic Church; and it left Tony wondering about the rules that religious institutions cling to in order to maintain control of the faithful, who in the end are driven from institutions they love because of rules they cannot accept.

Tony's friend joined a megachurch, one of the largest in central Ohio. At the outset, it was a small group, full of life and Christian love. "Then pretty soon we had to have rules and people in charge. You have to have this and that. We're ready to leave. It's just so political. Yeah, there's faith there, but you have to get around all the garbage to get to the faith," his friend lamented. Tony recognizes that Concord will get to that point, but he's not concerned about that, yet.

Rules seem to go hand in hand with issues of size. Written into Concord's founding document is the notion that once the congregation reaches 500 members, it will plant a new church. Tony is pleased about this idea. He is completely convinced that there is such a thing as "big enough," especially when it comes to a religious institution. He mentioned the World Harvest Church, on the east side of Columbus, pastored by Ron Parsley, who according to Tony is "real big into the political side—getting the Christian Right into political office."

Whether you're for it or not, that's not my point. This church, and you're talking about thousands of people coming to each service, how can you—you know we all worship in our own ways and that's great, I'm all for that—but how can you have an intimate relationship with 6 or 7,000 people around you? But how do you say that's wrong when the other option is don't go? So if they found their niche, God bless 'em. I'm all for it. But it is not where I want or need to be. Parsley has a completely—if he's truly faith and God focused—he has a completely different definition of ministry, but that's okay. I'm sure there is a need for that somewhere.

That Concord is meeting in a school does not seem to bother Tony either, although he readily admits that it does bother a lot people. And he understands their struggle. Having spent a significant part of his childhood at his grandmother's home—a tiny little house in Columbus, a home where his large, loving family still likes to gather—he understands home is a blessing to be treasured.

A family needs that base, and the congregation is nothing more than a big family really. I agree we need a place. Is the cafeteria of the elementary school that place? Probably not. But having just jumped from church to church to church over the last ten years, this is very comfortable to me right now.

Tony credits Ginny and some of the other community leaders with having done a tremendous job making the congregants aware that the church is really located in their hearts. It is not the sticks and bricks. Carrying the Spirit with them, the parishioners of Concord Presbyterian Church are comfortable whereever they go.

And that's kind of cool. Now unfortunately, the first generation and maybe the second generation is going to pick that up. They're going to have a church with them no matter where they go. But ultimately you want to get to 4 or 500 people, and that's going to be lost. That's just the way it is.

The personal relationship, whether it is with the Divine or with another believer, is the core of Tony's faith. Though he fondly recalls his dad, myriad aunts and uncles, and all the grandchildren kneeling with their beloved grandfather saying the rosary in the living room, Tony and Patti have always taught their daughters that prayer is more of a conversation with God. There may be times when you find yourself in a conversation and you do not hear the response. Sit still, Tony suggests, "You're probably not being quiet enough."

That's kind of how we've always taught our kids. I hope we're doing it right. It wasn't in the owner's manual.

Though his daughters are following radically different routes, the foundation of faith has been laid and is discussed openly, at times passionately among family members.

Tony's oldest daughter, Meghan, is an art student at the University of Cincinnati. The other day she said, "You know, dad, I don't necessarily go to church every weekend, but I feel more spiritual now than I've ever felt in my life." Tony was pleased.

His middle daughter, Kristin, is on a softball scholarship at a private Christian school north of Columbus, Mount Vernon Nazarene University.

Nobody in the family knew much about the Nazarenes before Kristin started there. They have found a fairly strict religious framework.

She's kind of following the flow up there, but she's well-grounded enough at home that she takes a pretty good perspective on things. I'm not saying they're right or wrong, but she has things to balance and consider. And her older and younger sisters certainly give her enough phone calls to, in their minds, keep her straight.

Last year (2004) on election day, Kristin came home to vote. Meghan had filled out an absentee ballot since she was in Cincinnati. Kristin was walking through the house in tears. Tony asked, "What in the world? What's wrong with you?"

She's like, "I don't want to talk about it." Well, that means you're going to talk about it some. I want to know what's going on. Meghan, my oldest daughter, had called to talk about who Kristin was voting for. And I thought, "Oh, no. This is going to be fun, but this is going to be ugly." And she said, "You know, dad, I'm at school and everybody is voting for George Bush. Everybody told me what he says and how he is for the Christians and everything and he's the right person and Kerry is almost the devil." And I said, "All right, well, what's this have to do with tears?" And she said, "Well, Meghan called and Meghan said how in the world can you vote for that bum? . . . yada, yada, yada." And she said, "Dad, he's the right person. Everyone at school told me." And I'm sitting there and I'm laughing to myself because my oldest daughter is down at a public school in the arts program, the most liberal portion of their program, and she's just being spoon-fed on Kerry. And my other daughter is at the most ultimate-conservative Christian school and she's getting spoon-fed on Bush. I said, "Well, Kristin, how much of this have you researched? How much have you done on your own?" And she said, "I don't have time. I'm busy studying and working on softball." She's on scholarship. "So you don't know what you're doing except what everyone else has told you. So all you've done is sold your vote to everyone else. The beauty of a democracy (and we're really a republic), but the beauty of this system we have is we're only as good as our efforts. The political parties prey on people's lack of effort or lack of research. So you're a hundred percent right, but you're a hundred percent wrong, and so is Meghan, 'cause I know Meghan hasn't researched it; she already told me. There's no reason to be upset. It's just that if you're going to be an active contributing citizen, you have a responsibility." It dried her up.

So Tony's oldest daughter is "spiritual" and sometimes attends the Newman Center down in Cincinnati. His middle daughter attends mandatory Bible study and chapel each day as part of her college curriculum. And Emily, his youngest, is involved in Young Life[3] and continues to play the keyboard at Concord "when she doesn't have to work." He and Patti take some comfort in the realization that all three are well-grounded not only in who they are, but where they fit in God's universe. With some guidance, they are developing the tools they need to make difficult decisions. But regardless of one's tools, some choices are just difficult. Tony's own decision in the controversial presidential election of 2004 had not been an easy one.

Walking into the voting booth I had not decided. I was torn on so many issues. Ultimately, with a great deal of question remaining in my heart and mind, I voted for Bush. I voted for Bush for only one reason: he had started the "war on terrorism," and I thought that his time pursuing this before the election was not enough to prove whether it was effective or not. In hindsight, it appears that it wasn't worth another four years, but at the time that was my sole separator of the two candidates and my only reason for voting for Bush.

Both candidates are Christian men. Both also have some beliefs that I do not necessarily follow and seem a bit contrary to their Christian beliefs. For example, Kerry was proabortion, where Bush was antiabortion in most cases. As it turns out, the "Christian Right," antiabortion, "pro-life" candidate has us in a heck of a mess in Iraq these days with thousands of murders, rapes, and killings—all in the name of "weapons of mass destruction," which appears to have been a politically driven ploy to drive up the price of oil and line a few political friends' pockets. I understand that Hussein was a tyrant, but the rest of the world told us not to enter into the conflict. They apparently knew or believed something that our leaders didn't.

Being a person of faith has a profound impact on Tony's political decisions.

My faith enters into my decision of how I vote, but not in a "What Would Jesus Do?" type of thought process for every decision I make. If I have to ask myself that type of question in my daily decision-making process or when I vote, then I haven't the Christian faith I need to survive and thrive as a parent, spouse, coworker, friend, voter…human being. I do pray for God's grace and guidance daily, but I rely on His teachings and His being the center of my life to guide me in my ways.

I'm looking for a candidate who is able to think for himself and who isn't controlled by a political machine or financial backers. I'm uncertain if these types of candidates exist anywhere, but it's what I look for.

Tony manages his professional life with the same easygoing manner that guides his personal life. He is a landscape architect. Though he is up-front about his religion and his politics, he seems to see no real need to get too worked up about either.

My partner in one business, he and I really don't talk politics at all. Every once in a while we'll talk about George W. and George W. being the biggest horse's butt that ever came along, but we don't really talk about it.

The other business we're involved in has four partners, and one partner talks a lot. His son just joined the navy. And I thought, "Why?" He just graduated boot camp last week, and I thought, "What part of Iraq don't you understand?" I count my blessing every day that I never had to register for the draft, nor was I ever involved in military service. I am thankful for that. I never had to make the real hard decision about which way to go. But I can't imagine choosing that in this environment, this political climate. They just announced we just had our 2,000th soldier killed in Iraq.

Tony's approach to religion is similar. The first Sunday Tony and Patti went to Concord he saw one of his partners with his wife at the service. The partner whose son is going into the navy also goes to Concord; in fact, Ginny married him and his wife. The other partner does not attend, but he is supportive. All four partners are on the church's building committee.

I think it's not enough that I have to put up with you guys five days a week, now I have to put up with you another night, too. Fortunately, we all get along very well together.

Tony does not want to be "preachy." He much prefers "to shut up and let my actions do the talking." If someone knows he is a Christian, then he believes he has probably done his job. Beyond the building-committee business or the week's sermon, there is not that much church talk in the office. But it is a "very Christian environment," even though "we don't have Christian music playing on the radio."

At church Tony has encountered very little, if any, political discussion. This realization perplexes him, and he begins to ponder some reasons. Perhaps it is the diversity of the congregation—there would be little common ground—or perhaps the group is just too small. Or perhaps it is that the core of the congregation is relatively young—high school and college age—and they simply are not focused on politics. None of these hypotheses seem to satisfy him completely.

Tony has always been drawn to an outwardly focused church. As a child he always admired people who went overseas as missionaries. His exposure to the Brown Franciscans and the mission purpose written into their charter—they went to Central America and to Africa—underscored his commitment to a socially active church.

At the same time he harbors a sort of healthy caution about mission work.

Down in Charleston there was a fella at our church. He was a young guy. And he always talked about going to inner-city Washington and pulling people out of dumpsters and stuff like that. He was from one of those blue-blood families of

Charleston—you're talking mega, megadollars. And I thought, "You know, it's easy to be a servant, a missionary, when you have a safety net."

Tony has never really felt called to overseas mission work himself. He wonders if everyone went to Africa or Central America, who would be left to take care of folks here? He does, however, have his own form of outreach, though he realizes that the type of "mission work" he has embraced will probably never be recognized in the light of Mother Teresa.

My three daughters have each played softball. And girls' softball has always had a little bit of a knock against it. I heard it in the press as recently as this morning. It's still considered to be full of lesbians and all the social ills that go with that sport. I think my charter in life is to be here and just be present, be part of God's presence to these kids. So, I teach them softball. Yes, I am having fun. But I'm also having a heck of an influence on some kids. And they turn around and they say, you know what, it doesn't have to be that way, it can be this way.

Maybe it's a cop-out. Maybe it's just too comfortable for me to leave. I don't know. How do you make that decision? I don't know. There's still a part of me that says I ought to go to Ethiopia or to Central America. And maybe someday I will. I don't think now is the time. I think now is the time to be a presence in my kids' lives.

For Tony the chance to put in a few good words has given meaning to his life, but he has also honed his listening skills. And he has heard some surprising things along the way, surprises that Tony has been willing and, more importantly, able to embrace when it really mattered. Tony is not afraid to change his mind. A former music minister during college, Tony has always subscribed to the old adage, one who sings, prays twice. A few weeks ago they sang "Amazing Grace" at church.

I can't get through that song without puddling up. When my oldest daughter was born, Patti was working. I was in graduate school. The baby was a little colicky and she was up at nights, crying and stuff. I would pull her up to my chest, and I would go into my bass voice and I would just sing "Amazing Grace" again and again and again. I would go through all the verses I could think of. . . . Arlo Guthrie sings "Amazing Grace." He sings a version of "Amazing Grace" and tells the story of John Newton, who wrote the hymn. His history's not quite accurate, but Arlo Guthrie can spin a story pretty well. John Newton was a slave-ship driver and on his way from Africa to America with a boat full of slaves. He realized what he was doing was wrong. He turned the ship around, went back to Africa, and freed the slaves. That's not true, but he was a slave-ship driver and he did have a conversion and he wrote this song. I think he wrote the song after he stopped running slaves. Arlo said anyone who can change their mind and do things right like that is a friend of mine. I just can't get through it. Every once *in a while I'll catch my breath and I'll sing a little, but then I'll start puddling up again. That's the Irishman. The story of the Irishman is that his bladder is right behind his eyes. It's true.*

By his own admission Tony was never brought up as a Bible reader. His family Bible had always been used to record important dates. Recently he has been intrigued by John's letters.

I always like the story of people criticizing him because all he writes about is love, love, love; and John responds, Well, what else is there? Yeah, that works.

Monty Harris headed directly to the kitchen with what could only be called a huge vat of candied sweet potatoes. It was his specialty, a recipe from his mother. He was up late the night before, but he makes this dish for all the church dinners. There is no telling what might happen if one day he just did not. His wife, Stephanye, gladly relinquished the culinary responsibility to her husband, especially where sweet potatoes were concerned. Monty knew exactly what he was doing. He was a seasoned part of the kitchen crew. Anyone watching him make his way around the kitchen this November Sunday morning and Stephanye, drinking her ice tea and socializing merrily before worship, would be surprised to learn that it had not always been this way. The couple was a relative newcomer to this community.

STEPHANYE HARRIS

The Story Is Yet to Come

Stephanye Harris's mother gave her only daughter lots of advice, but "be careful of cults" was the sum total of her counsel on the subject of religion, offered as Stephanye headed off to college in the mid-1970s. Throughout her childhood her parents moved a lot, making an affiliation with a particular religious group difficult. But her parents never felt the loss, convinced that "the church was taking a different route than they were."

By the time she was in seventh grade, Stephanye's parents had settled in Houston, Texas. Dissatisfied with the city's public schools, they enrolled their daughter in a Catholic girls' school where she remained through 12th grade. Attending the obligatory mass, at age 12, was Stephanye's first exposure to organized religion. She objected to the mandatory attendance requirement for two reasons: "I hated the blouses we had to wear on mass day, and I wasn't Catholic." She boldly, albeit futilely, approached the Mother Superior with her concerns.

In spite of her opposition, her experience was not wholly negative.

I remember when we'd go to chapel it felt very peaceful, really nice. I felt like it was a holy place. We were all allowed to participate in mass; but it was kind of following along, listening, more than a welcomed-in kind of feeling.

This religious environment posed some troubling questions for Stephanye, whose adolescent angst, unlike most of her peers, was not focused on her concerns and difficulties, but those of others. She was much more worried about eradicating world hunger or stemming the rising tide of racism than she was about the newest nail polish or diet plan. She entered the Sacred Heart Girls School in the early 1970s. She recalls being required to watch more than one antiabortion film, complete with dismembered babies, as the nuns assiduously tried to keep these girls from making *that* choice.

I remember they were talking in the class one day about the burning bush and what that was, and I said to the nun, "Do you believe everything in the Bible is exactly true?" One of the other girls got really upset and started crying. So I remember that experience. They had the kind of attitude that things will not be discussed. There was just a real rigid thing happening there. This was when the nuns were still wearing habits.

At an early age, Stephanye was disturbed by hypocrisy. The girls often went on field trips to visit ornate cathedrals and churches filled with elaborate statuary. Upon returning from one such trip, the girls were set to work preparing Thanksgiving baskets for the poor as the nuns lectured on the importance of giving to those in need. Stephanye approached one of the priests and questioned why so much was being spent on church buildings if it was so important to give to the poor?

I noticed the school I went to had some of the wealthiest people in the United States. I saw that and I thought, "Wow, why do you need this much?" I saw the kids getting their Jaguars for their 16th birthdays and all that as hypocrisy. Where was the peace for the children who are poor?

In college she dedicated herself to antiapartheid work. In a sociology class Stephanye designed a research project examining churches as a microcosm of society at large. Her case study was the Seventh-Day Adventist Church. She discovered a white congregation that was deeply committed to its mission work in Africa. At times its members gave sacrificially of their resources to support this overseas effort. Then she discovered a black Seventh-Day Adventist Church a mile and a half away from the white congregation. She asked the white congregation, "Why do the Seventh-Day Adventists have two churches a mile and a half from each other? They had nothing to say." Their silence validated Stephanye's growing uneasiness with organized religion.

Stephanye went on to earn a master's degree. She then worked as an out-patient mental-health therapist in community mental-health agencies for 11 years after which she joined a private practice as a family therapist. She married in 1982 and had two boys. Today, over 20 years later, she is part of a thriving group practice. Her boys are both in college, and she is still happily married to her loving husband. She is a well-educated, successful, charming, confident woman, except in the face of the Divine. Until recently, when she encountered religion, she cowered.

I felt like nothing—zero worth. It didn't matter that I'd spent my entire life caring for the poor, doing what I could to help people out of my own pocket, as well as at work. I was not...I didn't have that "fit-in" label, so I felt like I hadn't achieved anything. The Christian women I knew prayed beautifully, could quote scripture, and all that; and I'm telling myself, "keep your mouth shut."

Stephanye had, very early in life, developed a strong sense of ethics. As she grew older, this "sense" grew stronger. She was clear about what was right and what was wrong, and she had no problem acting on her convictions. What she did not have was much in the way of theology. By her own admission, "God was nowhere in my life." When she was pregnant she started "having stirrings, a strong sense of a higher power," which only intensified as her children matured.

A colleague invited her children to Vacation Bible School and Stephanye, eager to find some connection with the Divine, gladly let them attend. Then one afternoon her four-year-old came home very upset.

He said they taught him that sins are like booboos, sores inside the body that will never heal. So he was thinking his body was full of sores on the inside because he didn't follow directions....And I'm like "No." He didn't go back. But we went to their graduation ceremony. They were waving and saluting the Christian flag. It seemed cultish. So I got the message: "Avoid organized religion. It's a scary thing."

Stephanye's husband, Monty, had some health problems, and then the couple got busy raising their boys. Every once in a while she would think about finding someplace where her family could get involved. Sometimes they would get so far as to visit different churches in the community. For a variety of reasons, but "mostly because of the rules that the churches had," the Harris family did not find its place. Stephanye even gave the Catholic Church another try, but while sitting in the pew she read a seemingly simple request on the back of the bulletin: if you are not Catholic, please stay seated during communion. She was frustrated by the rules, by the all-too-familiar rigidity of the system. Religion seemed to be a little room with no way in. And yet, it was something she really wanted. She struggled to find her place, a way through the walls, which in her mind had grown into some sort of formidable fortification.

Along the way Stephanye became paralyzed by the pressure. She was convinced as she got older, the gap was widening between her and those who knew the way "into the little room." By now they had years of experience. Most of her peers were churched, and Stephanye became convinced that many of those people thought she was "a bad person because she had not found a church."

I would say, "I am acting Christian towards other people." But then I kept hearing, "If you don't go to church, it's a real problem."

Still she was open about her search, seeking wisdom and guidance from any and all potential sources. A Pentecostal friend gave her a different translation of the Bible, hoping she would find it easier to read. But Stephanye found it difficult to reconcile the wide variety of interpretations of the sacred text. She knew that some believers took the scriptures literally, and then there were "people who were way on the other side, worshipping the trees." She became confused trying to figure out where she fit in. Then in the midst of her inner battles, her soulful searches, life would happen. Her husband's health would deteriorate, her sons and/or her work would demand her attention and she would, for the moment, "let it go."

It was during one of these times when Stephanye had "let it go" that her younger son, Nick, started going to youth group at Concord Presbyterian Fellowship. He was invited to play cello at the Christmas Eve service in 2003. Stephanye and Monty decided to join Nick. They were curious about this community with which Nick was becoming involved. They liked the service, but it was Christmastime and they "didn't think a whole lot about it."

For the next few months, Nick kept pushing his parents to come back and "give it another try."

He said, "They're really cool, not like other people." So we started going some to Concord. Then the church had a trip to Florida that spring, a youth-group event. They had a place to stay, but they needed chaperones. I agreed to go. I thought this would give me a chance to check out some of these people and see if they were going to end up trying to give me rules. They didn't.

Gradually Stephanye and Monty began attending more activities at Concord. Stephanye was pleased about her involvement in the community, but she continued to be anxious about her inexperience. She was particularly worried about Bible study. She liked these people and she sensed that they liked her. She was afraid she would ruin everything.

Somehow I thought I had to be at a certain point in my own education before I would be able to attend a Bible study. Something kept at me to just go and try it, but I was a nervous wreck. Then I went. There was a young woman there asking questions that I was thinking, but was afraid to ask. I had a 45-year-old body; I'm not supposed to be asking these things. Slowly I started to get to know the congregation a little bit and feel more comfortable. "Okay, these people aren't rule based. They're not going to judge me." And then I started getting a sense that it's okay, you can love God and He'll accept you where you're at. And you can have a relationship with Him before you know all about Him. I'd never heard that before. I didn't know that.

In May 2005, a year and a half after Nick had played the cello on Christmas Eve, Stephanye and her husband chose to be baptized at Concord.

By that time, she knew she was in the right place. The elusive, exclusive little room had been replaced by an open-air sanctuary, literally and figuratively, since at the time Concord Presbyterian Fellowship had no sanctuary and was worshipping in a tent. Stephanye heard that Ginny was planning a service of baptism for newborn babies and adults who wanted to reaffirm their faith. As soon as she was aware of this service, Stephanye was certain she wanted to affirm her newfound faith; but she was afraid to ask. A few days before the service Stephanye was in Bible study and someone mentioned that an adult was planning to participate in the baptism. Stephanye was delighted by Ginny's reaction, "That would be cool." That night after the Bible study Stephanye told Monty that she was going to take part in the baptism. He said he wanted to also. So on Sunday, the two went up to the altar and confessed their faith before the congregation.

I was already pretty much in tears before I went up there. And during it I was like, "This is wild beyond belief." It was a sense of not wanting that feeling to ever change, that it would be like this forever. And it was a sense that my body wasn't important. My husband and son came up, but I wasn't even physically present, but I was. There was this overwhelming sense of being with God and this transcendence and I was like, "Wow, this is just. . . ." No sense of questioning, but it blew my mind at the same time. I didn't expect it. It was just a really, really wow feeling. And I thought I shouldn't mention this to anybody. It seemed like such a personal thing. It was such an intimate moment that I felt like it transcended my relationship with my husband, my children, with any person. It was a real private thing. So I didn't say anything, but I knew that a major change had just been in my life, that I had been forgiven. That I had been accepted. And that I had a lot of work to do. It's a big responsibility.

Stephanye had sought the blessing of so many Christians throughout her life. Now that she finally felt she had been accepted by God, the blessings of others—though abundant—really mattered very little. Stephanye does not regret those years spent searching.

I haven't had the sense that I should have done this earlier, because there wasn't a place to be. I just feel content where I am now. I know every day I wake up with God and that He's in my life and that's okay.

In fact, it is the very unique circumstance of Concord Presbyterian that made it possible for this place to become her place, to become Stephanye's place. The church is run by a woman. It is growing and vibrant. It is not traditional. There is no entrenched group of people telling others how it should be done. Everything is new. Stephanye does not miss having a traditional sanctuary, because that was never her tradition. What does matter to Stephanye is being part of the community. She deeply appreciates the time to come together, the shared ritual to celebrate each passing week and look forward to the blessings of the next.

As her faith developed, her prayer life became pivotal. Looking back, Stephanye wondered why some of the Christians friends she had encountered during her search did not encourage her to pray. "Maybe they thought I wasn't ready," she mused.

Ginny helped Stephanye learn to look for opportunities to pray. That summer the congregation was still meeting in the tent, their open-air sanctuary, and a fire truck and an emergency vehicle went by, sirens wailing. Stephanye recalls hoping that Ginny—who was in the middle of her sermon—would not be irritated by the interruption. On the contrary, Ginny stopped her sermon and prayed "for whatever's going on right now." Stephanye was surprised, and impressed.

I thought, "Wow, that's really cool." As I started hearing those messages I felt like my whole brain was opening up. I found myself not just being able to feel God's presence in the church, but I found myself starting to pray.

More and more Stephanye finds herself in prayer. Sometimes during her sessions as a therapist she asks for guidance, for the next session or even during sessions, "God, I am quiet right now, what do you want me to say? Or should I just be quiet right now?" She is finding times for God that she never expected; it's becoming more and more a part of her daily life.

She has been a therapist a long time, but only recently have her clients wanted to discuss God. One teenager asked her about the existence of God; another person wanted to talk about hell. Stephanye finds this development "totally bizarre," since "there's nothing different about me. I'm not dressing differently. I'm not talking differently. I don't have crosses plastered all over my office." For her part, Stephanye is the first to admit that she is not trained as a Christian counselor. She tries to respond to these heartfelt queries with general answers and then to answer only what her client is asking.

Stephanye is a little more direct, one might even say, blunt, with God.

I don't pray pretty prayers. It's just like, "Okay, God, I'm in the car and I've got my cigarette lit. What are we going to talk about on the way to work today? Please be there for me. I've got a busy day. You know what these people need. Please guide me. Please lead me. What do you want me to do?" Nothing pretty, just a conversation.

During her 45-minute drive to work she listens to Christian music and tries to use that time to explore her deepening relationship with God. Though she loves the energy of the contemporary Christian music, Stephanye has a profound connection to the old hymns. When she hears some of the old songs, she finds herself sitting on the church pew next to her grandmother. She enjoys looking at the copyright dates in the hymnal, recognizing that Christians have been singing some of these songs for hundreds of years. She relishes the connection with a tradition, with all those people who have sung the very same song so many times before.

"Amazing Grace" has a totally different message for me now. The message is: it has saved a wretch like me. I know I am forgiven. I know I have a purpose. I know I have a lot of work to do, and that's what I set my sights on.

Helping those in need had always been a part of her life. Sharing was second nature to this vivacious, empathetic woman. Stephanye noticed immediately that Concord was engaged locally as well as globally. She joins members of the congregation when they work at the New Life Food Pantry, distribute food and coats throughout Columbus to people who are homeless, and put flags on cars to honor returning soldiers. Twenty members, including Stephanye, attended the New Wilmington Missionary Conference and participated in the group's efforts to make disaster relief kits. The congregation has contributed to Darfur's needs and supported individual members on recent mission trips to Siberia and Ireland and has helped an Ethiopian family that received a diversity visa to settle in the Columbus area. Ginny Teitt, Concord's pastor, and three church members journeyed to Ethiopia to develop a cooperative plan to help develop the area's suffering schools.

Recently, Concord has felt called to move the Ethiopian family (that we helped to settle and continue to support financially) to our church family, so we are offering them part-time jobs within our church. We have secured housing nearby, and they are now attending our church. Under Ginny guidance, we discovered last month that they felt called to come to the United States to minister to "white people." We feel ourselves growing a diverse congregation.

This is the kind of church work Stephanye deems "really important," the kind of work she enthusiastically claims as *her* church work. There are the other efforts initiated under the banner of Christianity Stephanye finds troubling. She recalls a bumper sticker stating that the moral majority is neither. She has always been "kind of amused" by the prayer-in-school debate.

How can you separate church and state? The whole country was founded on it. I don't know what I'd do if someone came to me. I'd have to think about that and some of those things. But I am very clear on homosexuality. I have no reservations at all. I think they're made by God as well, and that's just the way it is.

Stephanye is one of those people who was just born with an innate sense of right and wrong. Now, as she becomes more confident in her faith, she is beginning to make theological connections as well.

We do not need to hide behind labels and stereotypes. The "church" has gotten away from Jesus' message. To walk in his image means to love everyone and include everyone. Don't judge, help. Serve. Do what Jesus would do in the situation. Don't condemn. Teach. Practice what you preach. I see folks who claim to know "the way" and if you don't do it "their way" you aren't included.

The connections between her newfound faith and her political choices remain to be seen. She prayerfully approaches the fall's upcoming elections.

I find voting intimidating and complicated. I can't say I have considered faith consciously since I haven't voted since my recent life-changing baptism.

In the face of the tragic aftermath of Hurricane Katrina, Stephanye saw no point in grappling with questions like, why would God let this happen? For her the message was that God wanted to get the attention of His people, to tell them that there are "more brothers and sisters that need to be taken care of."

So there are things happening. He's giving me guidance in ways that just blow my mind sometimes. Sometimes I get tired by the end of the day, but I just find that my whole life has improved so much since I've gotten His help and I'm trying to focus more on His plan and not mine, which is pretty hard to do. It's been really just since May, so for me there's not a whole lot of a story now; I think the story's yet to come.

The prayers had been prayed, and the songs had been sung. The Word had been preached. The benediction had been pronounced. The worship service was over, but not one person left. Instead people moved back the chairs and pulled out the tables. Three tables were placed end to end and after the colorful tablecloths came the food: green beans, broccoli, tossed salad, potato salad, corn bread, stuffing of all sorts, sweet potatoes, ham, and finally the deep-fried turkey. The desserts filled a table of their own.

Someone said a blessing and then it was feeding time in the cafeteria of the Eli Pitney Elementary School, but then again, maybe it always was.

4

Obedient to the Word: Second Baptist Church, Houston, Texas

Narrator: Moses, Aaron and all the people who left Egypt with them have been traveling for three months. They have seen incredible miracles of God.... Moses has been gone for five weeks. God is telling him the Ten Commandments and how to build a special tent for his people to worship Him in. He also is telling Moses a lot of other rules and laws that will help the people survive. Some of the travelers are beginning to wonder if Moses is going to return....[1]

The third-graders in Kellye Williams's Saturday evening Bible study were having a marvelous time digging through a large plastic box appropriately labeled "costumes." Many of the colorful robes and scarves they chose were too big for them—perhaps sometimes older youth or even adults adorned themselves with these biblical vestments—so one of the dads was busy folding or tying or wrapping their garments of choice around more than a dozen eight-year-olds who were members of the class.

Meanwhile Kellye was handing out scripts and assigning roles. She would read the part of narrator. The other speaking roles included Moses, his brother, Aaron, and two Bad People. The rest of the children would be Good People, Weak People, or nonspeaking Bad People. For the most part, these energetic but well-mannered kids did not seem to care which role they were given, although once it became clear that the Good People got to kill the Bad People at the end of the skit, a few of the children became more passionate about their preference.

After the group of third-graders practiced for a little more than 30 minutes, their audience arrived. Ten or 12 first-graders came down the hall to see the skit. Kellye, the poised and articulate narrator, began by explaining to the children about all the miraculous ways in which God had cared for the

Israelites on their journey out of Egypt. The scene opens as Moses tells his people God has summoned him to Mount Sinai, and Aaron will be in charge during his absence. Moses is gone for five weeks, and the Israelites become anxious. Bad Person #1 confronts Aaron:

> Aaron, we don't think your brother Moses is coming back. We want something we can trust in to lead us. That golden calf in Egypt always guided the people there. We want a golden calf too.[2]

Aaron directs the Bad People to gather all the Israelites' golden jewelry. The Bad People bring big plastic shopping bags ostensibly filled with the jewelry and place them at Aaron's feet. He fashions the precious metal into a calf, which in reality is a large yellow horse piñata. The first-graders are visibly amazed as the miraculous transformation takes place right before their eyes. When God informs Moses that Aaron, the Bad People, and the Weak People are worshipping the golden calf, Moses is furious. He returns to the people and tries to set things right, destroying the calf and making the transgressors drink a bitter drink of penance. After allowing sufficient time for some dramatic drinking and disgusted faces, Moses then commands:

> Anyone who is on the Lord's side, come stand beside me. (Good people move to be beside Moses. Moses pulls them away from the others and speaks to them.) The Lord wants you to use a sword against those who are still against him. (Good people pretend to stab the bad people; bad people fall down on the floor; weak people drag them off stage.)[3]

The narrator has the final word, reminding the actors and the audience alike that God will take care of those who are obedient to His Word.

> The Lord told Moses that He would send a plague. Many people who worshipped the calf died from the plague. God promised to send an angel to lead the rest of the people to the Promised Land. He promised to make it a safe place for them to live. He reminded them that He can be trusted.[4]

The skit was over. Some children bowed and some children clapped. The first-graders returned to their classroom, and the third-graders took off their robes and finished up their chocolate chip cookies and cups of blue juice.

As Kellye Williams gathers the crumpled scripts, tosses a few cookie wrappers into the trash, and cleans up some spilled juice, she can feel satisfied that this evening the third-grade class at Second Baptist Church has not only heard, but participated in the Word. They are learning biblical lessons that their creative and dedicated teacher and their appreciative parents are hoping will serve them well for the rest of their lives.

Kellye and her husband, Fred Williams, have been teaching a children's Bible study at Second Baptist for six years. They taught their son's, Preston, class when he began first grade and followed that class through the third grade. They began the process over again when their daughter, Courtney, entered first grade. So they are no strangers to children's Bible study. What is new for them is teaching on Saturday evenings. Second Baptist has grown so large—it now serves over 40,000 members on six different campuses—that a few of the classes were asked to switch to the Saturday evening hour in order to alleviate some of the overcrowding on Sunday mornings. The Williams agreed to make the shift since their son, now in junior high, was already at the church attending youth group on Saturday nights. The family is still getting used to its new routine: 5:00–6:00 P.M., Bible study; 6:00–7:00 P.M., worship; and 7:00 P.M., junior high youth group. Sunday mornings are uncharacteristically quiet at the Williams's home.

After cleaning up the classroom, Kellye drops her daughter off at JUMP—children's church—and then heads downstairs to the worship center. She arrives as the soloist is completing the first verse of "It Is Well With My Soul." The song seems somehow right for this lovely, penetrating woman.

When Kellye's son was about to be born, she and Fred prayerfully decided that she would leave her flourishing career at Exxon and stay at home and raise their family. This preference, which involved considerable financial adjustment for Fred and Kellye, was perplexing to many of their colleagues. Those at church needed no explanation: the young couple had chosen to make family a priority. Ironically that commitment was the reason Kellye was worshipping alone tonight. Fred, who is much more dedicated to nurturing a strong father-son relationship than he is to watching football, had nonetheless found a way to combine the two. He had taken their son to a University of Texas Longhorns vs. University of Oklahoma Sooner football game at the State Fair of Texas in Dallas. The pair made it a point to come home Saturday evening; they would attend worship on Sunday morning.

FRED WILLIAMS

Focused on His Family

My faith affects my choices. As a young boy I had an interest in politics and probably still have the bug. Some might say you're not going after your dream, but I've made a conscious decision not to. I thought I wanted to go into politics, but as I saw the toll it takes on people's lives, there is hardly a congressman or a U.S. senator that has not been touched by divorce. Your kids suffer because you're not there for a lot of their activities. And I just decided that for me, I want to be married for the rest of my life. I want to see my kids play soccer, football, baseball, piano, whatever they are involved in. I want to be there for them. My number one priority is to be a spiritual leader to my wife, a good husband and father to my kids.

I have a good career. I enjoy it. I work hard while I am at work, but once I leave the office, I enjoy being with my family. My career is there as a means to an end, *to support my family. Once you're focused, it's easy to make decisions. You know what to turn down and what to get involved with.*

Focused on his family is a plausible, but by no means inevitable, place for Fred Williams to find himself as he looks toward middle age. He is the president of a Houston-based trust company, an affiliate of an investment management firm that manages over $5.5 billion for a wide range of influential clients. He is a successful, well-connected businessman in one of the most vital, politically significant cities in the United States. He openly acknowledges his "love" of politics. And yet Fred has chosen piano recitals instead of politics. Having found his focus as a young adult, the choice was not difficult, but it was a choice.

Fred is a third-generation Baptist. He grew up in Corpus Christi, Texas, with his mother, father, and four younger sisters. The Williams family attended First Baptist Church. When Fred was 11 a Sunday School teacher at First Baptist led him to Christ, and he accepted Jesus as his Lord and Savior.

Then when he was in high school his parents had a tough time in their marriage, which ended in divorce. Church attendance waned for the struggling family. His mom occasionally took him and his sisters to different churches, but they never found another church home. Fred did not think much about his spiritual development, "Back then if we were not being made to go to church, we didn't go to church."

Fred joined a fraternity, not a church, when he got to the University of Texas at Austin. In the four years he attended the University of Texas he never once went to a Bible study. He found himself at church about once a month, but readily admits his religious participation was probably inspired more by his devotion to the person he was dating at the time than his devotion to the Lord.

In 1978 Fred graduated from college and accepted a job with an accounting firm in Houston.

I came to Houston on the Thursday before Labor Day. I was excited starting a job with a Big Eight public accounting firm. I thought, "Big city, this is going to be a lot of fun." My phone had been installed just a few hours. I had given the number to my dad and my mother. Well, my dad called my grandmother, and she in turn called her best friends here in Houston, Dr. and Mrs. Ross Dillon. Within four hours of me having a telephone, the Dillons called and said, "Fred, we'd like to have you over to dinner Saturday night." They were about 80 at the time. And I thought, "Oh, gosh. I'm not sure I want to do this." But I said, "Okay." I went because they had been such good friends with my grandmother. My grandmother was particularly a very strong Christian.

Fred's grandmother lived in San Antonio and though he saw her periodically throughout his college years, it was the visit three weeks before the beginning of his freshman year that stands out. Fred, not yet 19, was wrestling to finalize the financial arrangements for his studies. His grandmother sat down and prayed with him. Having lost her beloved husband ten years earlier, this faithful woman knew what it meant to feel alone and need help, but she also knew how it felt to be embraced by God's love and cloaked in His care. In the course of her prayer, she shared with Fred the numerous times God had come to her aid and taken care of her in times of need. As a young man Fred was moved by this encounter with his grandmother. Looking back almost 30 years later, he wonders if perhaps there was more than romance that motivated him to attend church, albeit sporadically, during his college years. Regardless, he is certain his grandmother was "planting seeds" that would help him find his focus not too many years hence.

They had finished dinner and Fred was about to leave, when the Dillons invited him to church the next morning. They were active members of Second Baptist Church and were eager to introduce Fred to their new pastor, Dr. Edwin Young. Dr. Young, who had been serving a church in South Carolina, had just arrived at Second Baptist three weeks earlier.

Fred really did not want to go. He had thought if and when he got around to attending church in Houston, he would go to First Baptist. But he needed to meet people and this was, after all, the Dillons inviting him, so he reluctantly joined the hospitable elderly couple the next day at Second Baptist Church. After the service, which Fred enjoyed, the Dillons insisted on introducing him to the pastor. Dr. Young offered to show Fred around the campus, which at the time was not nearly as extensive as it would become.

Dr. Young quickly gave me a vision of where they wanted to take the church. He explained that Houston was a young professional town, just filled with young professionals. And he said, "I would love for you to be involved and help us build that ministry." To make a long story short, I have never been to a worship service in another church in Houston, Texas, in the 28 years that I have lived here.

When Fred joined Second in the late 1970s there were over 1,000 members on the rolls, but less than 500 in attendance. The old sanctuary was less than half full. By the summer of 2006 worship attendance was averaging over 22,000 and membership was over 43,000. Fred feels privileged to have been a part of this exciting time of spiritual and numerical growth.

What attracted this somewhat hesitant young professional almost three decades ago is probably not unlike what attracts newcomers today. First, Dr. Young has a vision for the future of the ministry and a strong sense of mission. Second, the charismatic pastor enthusiastically "gives the ministry away." Unlike some other religious leaders Fred has encountered, Dr. Young insists that the ministry is "not all about him." Young readily shares his vision, trains his members, and invites them into the ministry "to be the salt and the light." And third, and perhaps most importantly, Second Baptist is a Bible-teaching church.

The mission claimed by the members of Second Baptist is uncomplicated and predictable: to lead as many people to Christ as they possibly can. In other words, this energetic congregation wholeheartedly embraces the Great Commission.[5] Many believe Dr. Young's vitality inspires his congregants to pursue their mission boldly. When they are thinking about the ministry, Dr. Young encourages the faithful not to limit themselves with financial constraints or with that age-old cry, "it has never been done *that* way before." Instead he urges them to use their spiritual gifts and to "dream outside the box." Dr. Young's exhortations have resonated with Fred and profoundly shaped the man he has become.

Inspired by the work of evangelist and best-selling author Dr. Bruce Wilkinson, Fred thinks of life in terms of a comfort zone and a cutting edge, poised on the brink of the comfort zone.

The closer I get to the edge of my comfort zone, the more uncomfortable I become. My first instinct is to retreat. But most spiritual growth occurs on the other side of that cutting edge. The further I allow myself to go beyond the edge, the more I allow God to use me. Inside the zone I'm comfortable because I am in control, but I am not really exercising my faith. On the other side of the edge, I grow because God is in control, not me.

According to Fred, Dr. Young's vision pushes the congregation beyond its comfort zone. As a church body, the members have learned to pray and then step out in faith, completely convinced that God is the one in charge.

There are some Baptist churches that are thrilling and alive, but others are on life support. In fact, the average Baptist church is probably 300–400 members, many smaller than that. Second Baptist has a vision for the least, the last, and the lost. Our church is very evangelistic. Everything we do has a hook in it to go out and lead people to Jesus Christ, whether it's through the Family Life Center, the softball or football fields, or our many activities and programs. Everything we do is designed to introduce people to Jesus Christ on a personal level.

Over the years Fred has been a part of tent revivals, softball and flag football teams, men's Bible studies at the Minute Maid Park (home of the Houston Astros), and joint services with other congregations. There have been singles weekends with speakers like well-known Christian apologist Josh McDowell, rodeo rivals, and Fourth of July parades and picnics, complete with fireworks in the field behind the church. Special services have honored the military, police officers, and firefighters. An exceptionally talented choir director composed a sophisticated, entertaining musical with a spiritual message. Every event is unapologetically designed to engage the participants in the Word of the Lord.

As a result of these activities, many people get involved and stay involved. Though Second Baptist boasts a large pastoral staff (numbering 33 on the Woodway Campus alone),[6] it is the participation of lay people, like Fred Williams, that causes the ministry to flourish. There is a generous spirit that reaches to the very core of this faith community. Those, like Fred, who have been around for awhile, feel no need to protect their place or position. Quite the contrary, they welcome newcomers with openness, almost delight.

The idea is to give the ministry away to people, to get them involved as quickly as possible. We want you to feel a part of the ministry and feel ownership.

The best way to "feel a part of it" at Second Baptist is to join a Bible study class, which Fred describes as "a church within a church."

You can attend here Saturday night or Sunday morning, and you'll sit next to some great folks. They'll introduce themselves to you and you'll think, "Boy, these are some nice people." But the odds of you sitting next to them again anytime soon are not very high. So we try to get you involved in a Bible study class as soon as we can, and that becomes your support group and your gateway to other ministries offered by the church.

But as important as the community-building component of the Bible study class may be, this pales in comparison to the real goal: Bible teaching. Bible teaching is what Second Baptist does.

We are encouraged to bring our Bibles to church and to Bible study. And they aren't just ornaments or decorations. They are going to be used. We are encouraged to write in them. Dr. Young will preach a sermon and say, "Write in the Bible. Mark it up. Get into the Word." He has always been a big believer in not taking a verse out of context. His sermons will typically include the passage: Who wrote it? When did he write it? What was the purpose? Who was he writing to? understanding the context around those particular verses. This is a church that you can count on knowing the Bible is not going to be ornamental, but is going to be studied.

Though steeped in Baptist tradition, it was not until he joined Second Baptist that Fred heard the term "daily quiet time." Congregants are strongly encouraged to spend 15 to 30 minutes each day in prayer and study. For most, including Fred, his Bible is at the heart of this precious time. Over the years during his quiet time, he has read through the Bible more than once. He generally finds a quiet place at home, not hard to do since he begins at about 5:30 A.M. and sits down with his Bible and a highlighter. He reads a

Psalm and a Proverb and then focuses on a particular Bible passage or sometimes a devotional book. He finds he is drawn to different texts at different
times.

*What I love about the Bible is that it's timeless. You can read a verse when you're
6 and it can mean one thing to you, and then you read it at 15, at 21, when you're
single, when you're married and have children. No matter where you are, it still
has meaning and is relevant to where you are today. I just love it. The more I read
the more I enjoy it.*

Fred also writes in a journal during his quiet time—a notebook where he
records his prayer requests and the date of the request. He prays for his family, for the president, the leaders of Congress—both the Senate and the House,
for wisdom. He also prays for his pastor, Dr. Young, and particular needs of
family and friends. Fred's wife, Kellye, is more of a night person, so the couple
has made it a priority to take a few minutes in the evening to pray together.
Although some nights it is not much more than five minutes, it has been very
helpful to their marriage.

Second Baptist has almost 14,000 people enrolled in weekly Bible study
classes. These classes are generally divided by age groups, but some classes
are topical or geared toward a particular group, such as single parents. Most
classes use a curriculum provided by the church. Typically in the Baptist
Church, and Second Baptist is no exception, the goal is to study the entire
Bible in a five-year period.

Classes last one hour, the first half hour of which is social, focusing on
announcements, community needs, and upcoming events. This is followed
by a half-hour lesson. Though it is never stated explicitly, there is an expecta-
tion that the teacher, a volunteer with no particular theological background,
will have prepared 10 to 15 hours over a two-week period before addressing
the class. Teaching the Bible at Second Baptist is a privilege and a serious
responsibility. Those who have accepted this obligation understand that.

Though the pastoral staff and other church leaders are constantly on the
lookout for new teachers, thus far they have had little trouble filling these
demanding positions. Fred observes that the Second Baptist community is
"particularly gifted." The congregation has attracted numerous people who
have been blessed with the ability to study and speak. And he is gratified that
even those who, like himself, have not previously had the opportunity to serve
in this capacity often find teaching is one of their gifts.

*For the first few years I was here, I was not a teacher. I'd really gotten out of . . . I
wasn't in the Word. I was involved in general. I was the social coordinator of my
Bible study class for a long time. My gift was putting the parties together. Then
after about four or five years they said, "You ought to try teaching." I'd been in a
men's Bible study; about ten of us met every week for about eight years. Through*

that I gained confidence to try teaching. I started teaching singles, then young marrieds, and then peers.

Though Fred enjoyed teaching adult Bible study classes, he and Kellye feel blessed to work with the children's Bible study at this point in their lives. Fred also teaches an annual four-week class for young marrieds at the church entitled, "Goals to Contentment/Financial Freedom: God's Perspective for Handling Your Money." He has designed a course that combines a biblical perspective on money with the expertise he has developed after almost 30 years in the finance industry. The premise of the course is straightforward: God's way of handling money is completely opposite of the world's way of handling money.

Fred confidently asserts that those who choose to manage their finances God's way can not only be debt-free, but will be blessed "beyond measure." He admits these blessings may not always be financial, they may pertain to some other area in one's life, but he urges the faithful to take God at His Word and test Him. It is Fred's contention that financial difficulties arise when people try to manage their resources "man's way" and not "God's way."

Following his own advice, when Fred and Kellye's children were ready for school, after much prayer, discussion, and more prayer, the couple decided to send their children to the local public school rather than the Christian private school at Second Baptist. Initially the impetus for their decision was financial; they were managing on only one salary.

They moved into a neighborhood that had exceptional public schools. Though they readily admit they neither have, nor seek, a "long-term game plan" regarding their children's education, thus far this family has been blessed.

We pray for one child at a time and take one year at a time. If one of our children needs something different, we will do something different (that is, private Christian schooling or home schooling). Our goal for our children is to see them flourish in their school experience.

Part of their prayer was that if they were to opt for public school God would use their presence in the school as a ministry tool. Educational standards are high, and parental involvement at their public school is exemplary. And God has opened the door for numerous ministry opportunities.

We invite people [to Second Baptist] all the time. We love the school here [at Second Baptist], and we're very supportive of it. But kids at Second Baptist School do not have as much opportunity to interact with non-Christian students who they can invite to various church activities. A few weeks ago Second Baptist had a junior high kickoff night. They brought in a speaker from Kanakuk Kamps in Missouri. My son invited eight friends. They had a great time.

Kellye has taken a leadership role in GAP (God Answers Prayers), a program at their children's school. The kids wear T-shirts with the GAP insignia once a month and have a gathering after school. They play games and have a lesson or a speaker. GAP is a Christian group, but it is not affiliated with any particular denomination or church. It is open to anyone who wants to join. The group meetings are divided by gender. Recent meetings attracted over 36 girls (out of Courtney's third-grade class of 48) and over 60 boys from Preston's middle school; all were public-school children.

Fred and Preston are also involved in a rather unconventional, but incredibly successful, ministry directed at junior high youth. Every Thursday morning kids from the nearby public middle school are invited to the local Whataburger ("slightly nicer than McDonald's") at 7:00 A.M. Parents drop them off. The kids have breakfast and then climb on a bus from Second Baptist Church. They have a brief, ten-minute devotional, are given a challenge for the day, and then the bus takes them off to school. At the location frequented by Fred and Preston 65 kids have been regularly feeding their ravenous appetites and equally hungry souls.

Fred is grateful his children rarely, if ever, find themselves in the position of having to defend their Christian faith. In fact, this faithful family has found quite the opposite. Courtney and Preston are comfortable praying or taking out their Bibles in school and participating in activities like GAP and the Whataburger breakfasts. Fred is well aware that this is not the case in other parts of the country. He suggests that Houston, with its numerous thriving churches, may be an anomaly.

We don't feel nearly as much persecution here in Houston as I believe exists in other parts of the country. As a Christian I am not bombarded in my everyday life with anti-Christian bias.

Knowing that he and his family are in a safe place is comforting to Fred, but he still feels a strong Christian obligation to work toward a society where more and more people are able to share that sense of sanctuary.

What I love about our church is I don't feel our church is judgmental from that standpoint [regarding questions in the church about abortion and homosexuality]. If you've messed up, come on in. No matter what you've done, come on in. We are all sinners, saved by grace. And we feel if you will immerse yourself in God's Word, God's Word and the Holy Spirit will do the work. My job is to get you here and be an encouragement to you and let the Holy Spirit do His work.

According to Fred the church will welcome sinners seeking redemption, but it will not ignore the sin. Fred rejects the notion that Christians can ignore the political controversies that divide them in pursuit of some sort of common ground. For this highly educated, thoughtful, astute businessman, that would simply be putting one's "head in the sand." Fred is a Christian.

My faith is who I am. I cannot make a decision about my marriage, my children, how I love my wife, how I love my kids, my profession, or my politics without my faith. It affects everything I do. It is who I am. I am a Christian, 24/7, 365 days a year.

Fred is a Christian and his Christianity shapes his politics.

I've grown as a Christian. The closer I get to God, the more black and white issues become. People talk about the gray areas. The deeper my relationship is with God, those gray areas eventually go away. When I was not as close to God, there were a lot more gray areas in my life.

When he makes his political decisions, Fred filters his choices through three lenses: Christian first, conservative second, and Republican third "and a distant third." He determines if a particular candidate is Christian and what moral values the individual espouses. However, Christianity is not a prerequisite for him: Fred might vote for a Jewish candidate; the important things are a person's values and the ability to lead. The values that are of utmost concern to Fred are the protection of life—from the unborn to the elderly—and the protection of the family.

He supports candidates and public policies that reflect these values. Fred is not rigid or unreasonable in applying his criteria, "If somebody's made a mistake in the past, I am certainly all for forgiveness as long as I've seen that they have changed." As he becomes closer to the Lord, Fred feels more able to assess a candidate's authenticity.

In President Bush's case whether you agree with his politics or not, I think he's a different person than he was as a young man and during his admitted abuse of alcohol. I think he realized that was a mistake, and he's turned his life around. Obviously to become president of the United States he has to have turned that around.

Fred is reassured having a man of faith in the White House.

Absolutely. It gives me comfort, if he sincerely means it, and I believe he does. Being in Texas, in Houston, I know people who know him well. You can pick out a fraud or a phony. I think he truly does pray. It gives me comfort that he's praying for wisdom to do the right thing. I sincerely think he is a person who is trying to do what he believes in his heart is the right thing.

Fred, in fact, is convinced that Christians throughout the United States are playing a vital stabilizing role in the society. He fears what would happen if this group were no longer able to function in this way.

Think about it. If you took all the Christians out of this country overnight, tonight all the Christians were just gone, what would happen to this country? It would be total chaos in 24 hours.

Fred is not a trained political analyst, but he is by no means unsophisticated in his assessment of society. He knows being a Christian may be helpful, but does not guarantee success nor ensure that sound political policies are being pursued. He admits that a Christian leader could end up appointing people who do not perform or make bad decisions. On the whole, Fred has been satisfied with President Bush (his failure to restrain spending being the one exception), particularly his decision to go to war in Iraq and the way the president is handling the aftermath of the conflict.

We're at war with the Islamofascists (is that the buzzword?). Democracy allows people to experience their individual God-given rights and the opportunity to flourish as a nation. The freedom provided by democracy will benefit the people of Iraq and Afghanistan, respecting their economies, their individual lives, and their children. They have been suppressed for so long. It has been the right thing to do.

Growing up, Fred's father taught his only son not to vote Republican or Democrat, but to vote for "the right man." But his Christian education, particularly his study of the Bible, has helped to diminish the gray areas with regard to political parties as well. He may be a Christian and a conservative first, but Fred is a loyal Republican with little patience for the policies of the Democratic Party.

The Republican Party is far from perfect, but it is the party that values life and fosters the culture of life. It fosters family values. How can a Christian vote Democratic with a party that leans so far left, allows abortion to happen—the killing of millions of babies—and promotes policies which harm the family?

As the Mark Foley scandal rocks a Republican Congress, Fred is the first to recognize that the Republican Party has no hold on moral values in the United States. He is frustrated by some of the disingenuous political leaders in the party. But he appreciates that Foley was removed from Congress immediately.

If somebody in the Republican Party misuses the public trust, I believe they need to be removed from office, no ifs, ands, or buts. Whereas in the Democratic Party

I don't feel this occurs so readily. If someone does something wrong, a double standard is often used. There is a distinct difference between the two parties.

Fred knows there are people in the United States who identify as Christians *and* as Democrats. He finds this baffling and has struggled to reconcile these seemingly incongruous belief systems.

Recently I asked a close friend whose opinion I value, "How can someone who says they're a strong Christian vote Democratic?" And they said, "There's a difference. There are people who really read the Bible and those that just claim they read the Bible. They say they're Christian....[There is a difference between] somebody that's sincerely acting, practicing, and seeking to draw closer to God and someone who pays lip service, never has a quiet time, never opens the Bible, hears an occasional sermon, and says, 'I'm a Christian.'"

This sentiment rings true for Fred, who maintains there is "absolutely no way I could vote for someone in the Democratic Party." He feels that party is simply too far off base on the issues of abortion, homosexuality, and policies that affect the family and national security. Although the amount of time Fred spends studying politics and political issues pales in comparison to the time he dedicates to family and Bible study, it is significant and he keeps well-informed.

He regularly reads two online briefings: "Tony Perkins' Washington Update," published by the Family Research Council[7] and another one from Gary Bauer, the chairman of the Campaign for Working Families.[8] Fred appreciates the quality of the information he receives from these sources and feels confident that "they are coming at it from the same perspective I am." He also follows the work of James Dobson, who spearheads *Focus on the Family,* a television and radio program broadcast on over 6,000 radio and 80 television stations nationally and internationally.

Fred respects Second Baptist's stance vis-à-vis politics: the church takes a moral, never a partisan, stance.

Dr. Young clearly states that we will never endorse a candidate, which we don't. We talk about the moral issues. This gives us the information we need to compare the voting records of the candidates.

Second Baptist does encourage voter registration on campus. Dr. Young believes it is a Christian's responsibility to vote, and Fred could not agree more, "I think if all Christians voted, we could strongly influence most elections across the country."

"I enjoy politics," Fred concedes. But he is also aware that not all people, especially not all Christians, share his enthusiasm. There are many who have grown weary of talking about abortion and homosexuality. Fred also sees fellow Christians who are busy raising their kids, keeping their own lives together; they do not have the time or inclination to get involved in politics. His mentor, Skip McBride, is one such person. "Skip is who I go to for counseling and wisdom."

SKIP MCBRIDE

A Living Faith

I am not actively involved in politics. In fact, I am very disappointed with politicians. With most politicians there is no real way to know their heart. Just because somebody voted right does not make him or her a good person. The Republicans may vote the way I would vote, but they may well be corrupt inside. Still I am pretty much a straight-ticket Republican voter because of the Democratic stance on social issues: promotion of abortion rights and the homosexual agenda.

Skip McBride considers it (for him) a "waste of his time" to involve himself in things political. He is convinced the Lord is asking him "to do other things. The Lord has not led me in that direction [toward politics]; I just don't have time." He has written a few small checks "and that's it." For the most part this jovial, white-haired man prefers to share his financial blessings with evangelists working throughout Africa and the Philippines. He smiles as he notes that "heaven is going to look pretty brown." In the end, Skip concedes that he could "care less" about politics, other than voting.

It is not that Skip believes the world is perfect; he is no stranger to adversity. He just looks to places other than politics, and to figures other than politicians, for solace, insight, assistance, and transformation. As a much younger man, he tragically lost his 18-year-old brother. More recently, Skip's mother was diagnosed with Alzheimer's. One of his grandchildren suffers from a fairly serious case of asthma. But somehow his world makes sense.

I can't figure out Iraq or the next election. But then I don't have to. The Kingdom takes the problem away.

Skip is a fan of "shoot 'em up movies." He does not drink alcohol, because he did not want either of his two daughters to engage in this behavior before they became of legal age, and it would have been disingenuous for him to do so. With his tongue pushed far into his cheek, this merry man describes himself as a "beat up, ol' sore-back lawyer." In fact, Skip McBride (whose real name is Ralph) is a partner in the Houston-based law firm Bracewell & Giuliani. This firm gained considerable prominence in many political as well as legal circles when former New York City mayor Rudolph Giuliani joined the firm as a name partner in 2005.

Skip was raised in the 1940s in a small east-Texas community. He grew up in the church "as did anyone in the area at that time." When he was 13 he understood that he was a sinner and accepted Christ in the First Christian Church. He remained active in the church throughout his youth. However, when he got to college, Baylor University, he became "a typical college kid," what some might call a "C and E" Christian, attending church only on Christmas and Easter. He continued along that path until he finished graduate school.

If you knew me then, you would not think I was a Christian because I sure didn't live like one.

In 1970, after completing law school, also at Baylor University, Skip moved to Houston with his wife and two children. Having done exceptionally well at school, he was offered an enviable job with a large, prestigious law firm. The McBrides joined Second Baptist a few years before Dr. Young—who would in the years to come emerge as not only his primary spiritual guide, but also as one of Skip's favorite golf partners—arrived in Houston. Skip's daughters attended Second Baptist School, and his wife became involved in Bible study. This wholesome, young family was comfortable and contented as they made Houston into their home, but Skip is the first to admit at that time he "was not intimate with the Lord." He considered himself a Christian, but some 30 years later, he recognizes, he still was not living like one.

Then a friend at a law firm invited him to Bible Study Fellowship[9] and for the first time Skip began really reading and studying the Bible. He read the Bible, in its entirety. The Word of the Lord became real for him. He felt as if a "hazy focus" had somehow been "illuminated." Simply put, Skip explains, "Before I knew about God; now I knew God." The transformation was not dramatic. He cannot pinpoint exactly when the change took place, but that is inconsequential. For Skip what matters is that his life is different.

With his focus on Bible study came a commitment to an active prayer life. Skip's intellectual and spiritual energy, which previously had no outlet other than his academic studies, or later, his professional work, nourished his vibrant spiritual growth. Prayer life became a priority. Skip spends one hour each morning in quiet time.

In private study is where it all begins. I have found there is very little opportunity for growth without it. I do it alone, because I am a pray-out-loud kind of pray-er. I don't hear voices in response, but I receive guidance, a sense of the route to go. I pray about every decision, every meeting. No matter what it is, I bathe it in prayer.

Songs or music are never a part of his quiet time. "I am not into music." But the Bible figures prominently. Two verses stand out: Genesis 1:1, "In the beginning *God*. . ." (Skip's emphasis added), and Romans 8:28, "We know that all things work together for good for those who love God, who are called according to his purpose." Though Skip claims he is still a "great sinner and fails regularly," he can no longer claim "you would not think I was a Christian because I sure didn't live like one."

At the law firm Skip has a regular devotional gathering with his team. He tries to surround himself with people who share his Christian values. When he hires young lawyers he considers character to be of the utmost importance. Skip is very clear that money, prestige, and security, what the law firm and the world have to offer, are temporary. What he tries to do in a "winsome, thoughtful, nonprovocative way" with clients and colleagues alike is help them to see "what the Lord has to offer them is permanent."

Skip readily acknowledges in today's world many would label him a right-wing fundamentalist. However, he predicts that in ten years' time it is the mainline Protestant, perhaps even an Episcopalian, to whom society will assign the right-wing fundamentalist label. In other words, Skip forsees a public trend that is increasingly antichurch and anti-Christianity. Christians will be pushed further and further into the background. He recounts an experience at his law firm last December when Skip pushed long and hard before the firm consented to send some cards wishing colleagues and friends a "Merry Christmas" rather than "Happy Holidays." Skip realizes the Lord has blessed him with good cases and a rewarding career, but there is no doubt his relationship with God takes precedence over his relationship with the law firm.

The way in which Skip interprets his baptism illustrates his basic approach to faith. His baptism is not a condition to being Christian. It is a symbolic declaration of his acceptance of Christ as his Lord and Savior. Walking down that aisle is a conscious, outward display that says to the world, "I am not ashamed of the Gospel."

Throughout the years, participating in the ministry at Second Baptist has played a significant role in Skip's life. He has felt called to work with young married adults, particularly the men. It was here Skip first encountered Fred Williams. Teaching Bible study for these young men, Skip was able to incorporate issues of marriage, affluence, and child rearing, underscoring again and again that "God's way is the right way."

The theological premise that guides Skip's life and that he wants to share is not complicated:

There is a heaven. There is a hell. I have accepted Christ and will spend eternity with Him. That is the point.

Although he is boisterous and always ready for the next joke, Skip is also somehow calm, even at peace. He exudes contentment, with good reason.

My goal has already been achieved. When my kids accepted Christ, I finished my job. Oh, of course I still help them, and we have plenty of issues. But I know the main issue has been solved. Everything is taken care of.

An older couple got out of the car. It was already well over 80°F on this particular Sunday morning, but he was wearing a jacket. They walked, hand-in-hand, through the expansive, and nearly full, parking lot to the side door of Second Baptist's Worship Center. Once inside they headed down the carpeted, air-conditioned hallway toward the Choir Room. The woman, who seemed to have been treated kindly by the passing years, turned to go in; but before her good-natured spouse dropped her hand, he gave her a kiss and said, "Sing 'purty.'"

It was still at least 30 minutes before the 9:30 A.M. service—the one many at Second Baptist refer to as "traditional"—was to begin, but the sanctuary, which seats over 5,000, was becoming crowded. Rather contemplative organ music could have peacefully filled the handsome space had those gathering not been quite so enthusiastic in their greetings. A cameraman clad in black, right down to his leather boots, prepared his equipment to televise Dr. Young's sermon. The day's message would be aired not only at other Second Baptist campuses, but throughout Houston, other parts of Texas, the United States, and North America.

In the front of the sanctuary, two large screens flanked an intricate stained-glass window depicting a cross on a hill and a small lamb illuminated by the light from the empty tomb. The images on the screens faded from devotional images of crosses into notices about the availability of child care and reminders to turn off cell phones, back into crosses, and then into promotional announcements for upcoming concerts and special worship events. Gradually the meditative images returned, and the orchestra began to play. People were aware that the service was beginning, but it was as if their verbal exchanges were also an honored part of worship and could not be short-changed. Any one of these gathered could have stayed at home and watched this very service on television in the privacy of his or her own living room. Each had chosen instead to be present as part of the community.

After the call to worship and the opening prayer, the lives of literally scores of infants were dedicated to the Lord. Visitors were welcomed and then came the adult baptisms. The baptismal pool, located directly below the central stained glass window, was illumined, and eight adults donned white gowns and participated in this ritual symbolizing their new identity in Jesus Christ.

JACK LITTLE

Finding the Way Home

We were all baptized in the little First Baptist Church in Mandeville, Louisiana, on the same Sunday evening. Our daughter would have been about 16, and our son would have been about 13. It was a big thing. I grew up in a church that had infant baptism. But then I came to realize baptism was an outward expression of my faith. I would like to think seeing my wife and me being baptized would mean something to my children. For us, switching from one Protestant faith to another, my children had a chance to see it. It was quite an experience, one I will never forget. I was pretty nervous. Everybody out there in the congregation had already been through it. It was a very warm friendly group of people.

Now in Second Baptist, with 6,000 people sitting out there on Sunday morning, that's really something. Edwin [Dr. Young] said about two Sundays ago that this church baptized more than 2,000 people last year.

Jack Little grew up in the Methodist Church. His great grandfather was a circuit rider in east Texas, riding from town to town on horseback preaching and offering pastoral counsel along the way. Jack's father was raised a Methodist. His mother was a Baptist, but when the couple married, she changed her affiliation. So Jack grew up in the Methodist Church. Jack's wife, Carolyn, was a Methodist. They married in the Methodist Church and raised their children in the Methodist Church—at least initially.

Now retired, Jack had a successful professional life with the Shell Oil Company, ending his career as the company's president and chief executive officer. His work required that he and his family move around quite a bit. The Littles lived in Texas, California, Louisiana, and London, England. In the early 1970s this somewhat peripatetic family was living in Houston. They bought a house in a newly developing suburb on the north side of town. Jack recalls, "Everybody there was in a brand-new home. We were all about the same age, raising our kids."

A new Methodist church was being established in the area. The Littles were Methodist, so they joined the venture and helped raise money to build the first permanent buildings on the chosen site. The church, which had been meeting in a community center, was soon blessed with a lovely sanctuary. But in spite of the tremendous resources—financial and otherwise—Jack and Carolyn dedicated to this community, after a few years they had to admit the Methodist Church was not meeting their needs.

They just weren't teaching the Bible. I wasn't pleased with the direction the church was going. We were trying to raise our two young children, and we didn't feel they were getting the kind of biblical background they needed.

At this time Jack's office was located in downtown Houston, about a block from the First Baptist Church. The widely acclaimed Rev. John Bisagno held a noontime Bible study once a week. And Jack decided to go.

Nobody invited me; I just heard about it. I don't even know how I heard about it. I got out and walked around a lot during lunch hour. I may have seen a sign that he had a Bible study, and I just dropped in one day. And it kind of blew me away. There must have been 200 people in there. They served lunch. I don't think they charged for the lunch. It was kind of an outreach thing. Rev. Bisagno got up and led a couple of hymns. He has a great voice. He could've been a professional singer. And then he just started talking, from the Bible. You know, I looked around the room and there were men, women, people like me in there.

Jack was not ashamed or embarrassed of his faith, but neither was he one to carry his Bible around the office or attend Bible studies and devotional meetings at work. He did his very best to live an exemplary Christian life, and by all accounts he was quite successful. Being in First Baptist Church with other professional people for a truly inspiring Bible study touched him. He went home and told Carolyn about his experience. She was intrigued. Jack continued to attend the weekly studies. And the couple prayed they would find a spiritual home.

A few months later they learned their minister at the Methodist church was seeking a divorce. This served only to increase the Littles' discomfort. They wondered how a pastor could counsel their children on the sanctity of marriage if he were embroiled in his own divorce. No matter how much they prayed, "It just didn't seem right."

So they decided to try a Baptist church in the area not far from their home. They attended Sunday School at the Methodist church, grabbed their kids, and went to worship at the Baptist church. Their children were not pleased about the disruption of their social lives, which by now were firmly rooted in the Methodist church. Even though a number of their neighbors were there, the Baptist church seemed somewhat strange to the Little family. There was a lot of singing and the service was livelier than the worship to which they were accustomed. But they were looking for a change.

We really liked it. More important than anything, it was biblically based. So we went to that church.

Before the Littles had a chance to join, Jack was transferred to New Orleans. They bought a house in a little bedroom community north of Lake Pontchartrain called Mandeville, where a lot of other oil people lived. It was not their first move. They had a routine: new place, find a new church. The first church they visited was the Methodist, the second was the Baptist. They chose the latter.

I guess it was a natural reaction on our part. We had not yet made a final decision to leave the Methodist Church. We were in the middle of that debate in
the family when I was transferred to New Orleans. So we tried the Methodist
Church first. I think by this time we really knew down deep that if we were going
to be happy, we would have to make what seemed, at the time, to be such a big
leap and join the Baptist Church. The First Baptist Church in Mandeville was a
perfect fit for us at that time. I know God led our family to it. It was small. Everyone knew everyone else. The Bible was taught in a fundamental, conservative way.
There was a strong Christian fellowship among the members, a perfect environment for our family.

It was there that the Little family was baptized, for the second time. Jack
has warm memories of that small, white frame country church, even though
he and his family were there only for a few years.

After New Orleans it was back to Houston. The Littles considered joining
First Baptist Church, but their daughter had just started to drive and these
proud yet realistic parents were reluctant to have their oldest child traveling
on the freeway in the evenings, as she would inevitably have to do when she
became involved with the church's various youth activities. So Jack and Carolyn chose a Baptist church closer to home and became very active. Carolyn
taught Sunday School and Bible study and her children, now teenagers,
enjoyed the youth programs. The Littles were at that church for about three
years, but something was not quite right: "Things just seemed kind of static,
status quo. It didn't seem to be really on fire. So sometime in the early '80s
Carolyn and I decided to come down to Second Baptist to visit."

Jack and Carolyn liked worship at Second Baptist. So they would attend
Sunday School at their local Baptist church and then rush down arriving just
in time for the service at Second Baptist. They juggled their Sunday mornings
like this for awhile, all the time praying for guidance and a church home.
Then Jack was transferred to London. Carolyn stayed in Houston so their
son could complete high school. Their daughter was already in college. In
London, Jack found his way to the American Church in London, "which was
made up primarily of people in the oil business who were on assignment in
London." He enjoyed the diversity of worshipping with Catholics, Methodists, Episcopalians, and Baptists. But he also stayed closely connected to Second Baptist, listening to weekly tape recordings of Dr. Young's sermons.
When he returned, Jack and Carolyn transferred their membership to Second
Baptist. They are convinced, "being members of this church is probably one
of the best things that ever happened to us." They had found their home.

My wife has been a Bible study teacher here almost continuously since we joined.
Our daughter and her husband met in the Singles ministry at Second Baptist.
Both of our children were married here, by Edwin. Our son's three children go to
Second Baptist School. We've been members of this church now for 21 years.

It's the longest we've been anywhere—primarily because we did move around a lot as a young family. It has just meant so much in the life of our family, our children, our grandchildren. This is our church home.

What Carolyn and Jack Little were looking for was a vigorous, conservative Southern Baptist Church. They are comfortable with Dr. Young's theology: "Edwin believes and preaches in the inerrancy of the Bible. That is something my wife and I agree with."

Second Baptist is a church that takes Bible study seriously. Jack muses that he has been through every book of the Bible since he began attending Second Baptist, some of them more than once. He appreciates Dr. Young's biblically focused sermons, noting Dr. Young's affinity for the books of Romans and Revelation. It occurs to Jack that he may have heard his esteemed spiritual leader pontificate on some of the passages of these books more than once as well.

Three of Jack's grandchildren attend Second Baptist School, and parents and grandparents alike are pleased with their educational choice. The academic environment is excellent and the education is Christian. Confessing that he may not be "up to speed" on all the details of his grandchildren's education, this obviously proud grandfather does wax poetic about the ten-year-old's Little League achievements as part of the Second Baptist team, noting that the young man's teammates were all Christians who shared his grandson's values. Jack also describes a Halloween celebration in which the children will be involved. "It is some sort of a party here that won't stress the mask and all that stuff, the pagan side of the holiday." Jack may not be familiar with the specifics, but he does know his son and daughter-in-law are getting what they want for their children.

They get biblical fundamentals while they are here at school. And I think that's fine for a private school. If you're paying for it and that's what you want, I see nothing wrong with it.

Jack recognizes that as his grandchildren get older, they will have to "deal with the real world." He knows that may pose some challenges, but it is his prayer that these children will have a firm foundation, strong enough to "carry them through."

In large part it is the Christian home that forges that foundation. Jack is convinced that the "fundamental element" of a strong Christian home is a strong marriage. When Carolyn and Jack were married, they pledged before God to accept a lifelong commitment to each other. Regular church attendance has been a part of their lives since their courtship. Much of their social life has centered around church activities. Their children grew up in the church and in the faith.

We always said grace before meals. When our children were young, we prayed with them at night before they went to bed. We've always tried to make that a central part of our lives. I am happy to say both of our children and their spouses are very devoted to the church, to one another, and to their kids. They have Christian homes. I hope that is something we helped spark.

Carolyn worked for a few years while Jack was in graduate school, but only until their first child was born. At that point they agreed she would stay home.

We both felt her place was in the home. We felt she needed to be with our daughter and, of course, she wanted to be. So she never worked, even after the kids went to school. I didn't want her to. First of all, she didn't need to. So I was very happy she didn't want to. She was satisfied with her life, our home, our kids, and her other activities. She didn't feel she had to go to work to find relief, an escape, or an avenue to do other things to get fulfilled. She didn't need that. Our daughter was working up to the time her first child was born, but she never worked after that. The same is true for our daughter-in-law. Our home and our children's in-laws' homes were the same way. And you can see it in those grandchildren. The mother being there all the time makes a difference.

Jack describes his wife as the spiritual guide in the Little family, and he is sure his children would agree. When it comes to decision making, this devoted husband strives for equality, talking through all important decisions with his God-centered wife. There are times when his wife willingly acknowledges Jack's expertise and thus shares her opinion, but allows him to make the final decisions. As they have grown older Jack observes they spend more time talking and enjoying each other's companionship, maybe because now that he is retired they simply have more time. (Jack and Carolyn have enjoyed traveling in the last few years, including 2 trips around the world and 16 additional trips abroad.)

Prayer always has been serious to Jack and Carolyn, not just before meals or at their children's bedtime. They each set aside time to pray, even during busy days. And when they are faced with difficult issues or concerns, they pray about them together. Jack recalls one time when he was still working and was less than ten years away from retirement.

I had spent almost three years in London in the early '80s when our son was in high school. It was not an easy time to go over there. But working for a company like Shell, it was a great opportunity. And it's the kind of thing if you don't do it you probably stymied yourself on the corporate ladder. So I went over there. I paid my dues, I thought, and I came back to Houston. I'd been back about five or six years, and they offered me a very good job to go back overseas to The Hague. Our son was in law school. Our daughter was married. I just couldn't believe it. I told them I would have to think about this, really think about it. I took 30 days. We prayed the whole time. To make matters more complicated, we had moved my wife's mother here to Houston. She was living in a retirement home and not doing well. And I knew it was going to be difficult on my wife to go off and leave her mother here, with nobody to look after her.

They prayed about the decision until the day came when Jack had to talk with the president of the company. When he left the house that morning he told Carolyn he thought he would have to say yes. She said she understood. Jack arrived at the office at the usual time, about 7:30 A.M. He had been at his desk less than an hour when the phone rang. It was Carolyn. She asked if Jack had spoken with his boss. Jack explained the meeting was at 10:00 A.M.

She said, "Well, our son just called." He said, "Mom, you know I really hate to see you and dad go." I think he broke down with my wife. He said, "I just hate to see ya'll go." You know I prayed about this decision and I didn't get any magic answer from the Lord, but I think the Lord was answering my prayer through my son, telling me it's really important for my family to stay together. I think my son was telling me, "You know, Dad, we just don't want this family broken up." I think God answered my prayer and my wife's prayers through my son calling my wife that morning. She called me and got me before my 10:00 appointment. I said, "Okay, we're not going." I went in there and told them. That was a major thing in my life. I know God answered that prayer.

God had answered Jack Little's prayer and made it clear to one of the most successful businessmen in the United States just how important his family was. Jack heard God's message and heeded His call not to go out to a foreign land, but to stay home. In the end, the decision was not really all that difficult. Once this faithful, honest man knew what God wanted, Jack was more than willing to comply.

Throughout his life Jack has tried to live in accordance with God's will. He is the first to acknowledge that he is a man with very strong beliefs about the way people should behave, live, and treat each other. He believes people should care for one another. Those to whom much has been given need to share with those who have less. Jack recognizes he and his family have been blessed with good fortune, and he actively seeks to apportion his blessings to others.

Ever since Carolyn and I were married, we have tithed to whatever church we attended. At Second Baptist we have a tithe-plus program we adhere to. That is our main way of sharing with others who have less. In addition, both Carolyn and I have been involved in philanthropic giving to charities outside the church, including supporting them with our commitments of time.

For Jack this is a way of sharing the bounty of his faith and extending the faith community. Likewise, Jack believes there are times when the church is called to extend or share itself, to play a prophetic role in society, and to be the voice of morality. For example, the church must take a stand on particular issues, like abortion. There is no doubt in Jack's mind that Second Baptist has willingly and effectively sounded its voice on this vital issue. Dr. Young and the congregation of Second Baptist are staunchly pro-life.[10]

It's been preached from the pulpit. And anybody who reads the Bible and believes what the Bible says would know, even if it weren't preached. The church plays a very important role. But the church must be biblically based when it begins to teach and preach. If it goes off and gets away from the Bible and just starts espousing political views, I think that's wrong. I don't support that.

Jack also believes the church needs to speak out on the issue of homosexuality. Again, he finds the teaching of Second Baptist to be clear, straightforward, and rooted in the Bible. In his book *Culture Wars: The Battle for the Next Generation,* Dr. Young explains his position:

> Homosexuality will not send you to hell any more than being a heterosexual will get you to heaven...How do our names get written in the Book of Life? When we confess our sin, repent of our sin, and receive Jesus Christ into our lives... It is a myth that homosexuality is natural and normal to some...To this day, there has not been a definitive, scientific cause shown for homosexuality. And even if there was, it would still be wrong...God gives us the ability to live a pure life of restraint...The idea that natural desires demand expression is contrary to life and contrary to biblical principles.[11]

Seeing very little room for theological flexibility, Jack, this gentle, affable grandfather, admits to being bothered by those within the Christian faith who embrace homosexuality.

I just don't know how they can come up with this interpretation. When I look at the Bible and read what it says, there is no way I can get to where they are. I've kind of wondered how they come up with this. How you can be a Christian and believe in abortion, not have a problem with homosexuality, commit adultery, and all those sort of things? How do you do that and still say you believe in Jesus Christ and his saving grace? I don't know. It's not for me to judge. I try not to do that, but I'm very confused. How could you have those sorts of moral values and still call yourself a Christian? It bothers me.

A compassionate man, Jack hopes others might discover what he has found in the church: "a refuge for people who need help." For Jack the church is a place where those who call themselves Christian can come at anytime and "be refueled."

Jack concedes, "I am not one who walks around with a whole bunch of Bible verses in my mind. Some people are very good at that, but that's just not my thing." But at the mention of music, he lights up.

I guess I'm just too old fashioned, but some of this Christian music now, I can't get with it. I prefer the old hymns. I really love those old hymns. While the offering is being taken the music director will lead the congregation in two or three songs. Usually those will be the old ones, the ones that people almost know by heart. Of course my favorite is "How Great Thou Art." That is my all-time favorite song. "Amazing Grace" and "Great Is Thy Faithfulness" are two other favorites. I want all of those sung at my funeral. "Onward Christian Soldiers" is a great song. I remember the song at my grandfather's funeral, "Rock of Ages." I've got a lot of favorite songs.

What these old hymns do for Jack is help create that place of refuge, that place of spiritual well-being, the place that Jack believes the church has an evangelical responsibility to share with others. Jack contends that Christians, those who have heard and accepted the message of the Gospels, must reach out to those who are not yet believers. Over the years, having watched any number of conservative Christian television programs, Jack figures there is "a right way and a wrong way to do this."

I think the way we do it, making Dr. Young's messages available on TV, you can turn it off. It's not in your face. If you hear something you like, you can listen to it. If you don't, switch to the cartoons. I think that's the right way to do it.

That said, Jack realizes the church is facing serious threats which, at times, demand an equally serious defense.

The church is definitely under attack. I think that's Satan at work in this world, trying to tear down the values the church stands for. There is a movement out there. Certainly the very liberal left-wing part of the political fabric in this country is trying to tear down the church because they see the church as something that espouses values they totally disagree with. They are always trying to belittle or make fun of people who have strong religious views and to denigrate people of faith who believe in God and believe what the Bible says is true. Those are the enemies of the church.

Jack contends that homosexuality and abortion are being used to divide the Christian community. Although he recognizes the formidable challenge, Jack insists the church's evangelical responsibility must extend into this arena as well.

I think that is Satan at work. And it's incumbent on the parts that don't believe in these things to do more and more to try and win people back to more fundamental biblically based teachings.

For some conservative Christians, insinuating themselves and their religious communities in the political process is the logical extension of this need to "win people back" and defend their church against its liberal enemies. This is not so at Second Baptist. Jack agrees with Dr. Young's approach: encouraging his flock to vote, placing the issues within a biblical context, but never endorsing a particular candidate or telling the faithful *how* to vote.

I don't think the church ought to be telling people how to vote. I think the church ought to frame the issues based on biblical principles, but leave it to the individual to determine how to vote. Now if they choose to vote opposite of the way the church is teaching, and the church is based on strong fundamental biblical principles, then they've got to answer to God for how they voted.

After listening to the folks at Second Baptist and doing much of his own reading and other research, Jack has chosen to support President George W. Bush, a Christian who believes he is doing God's will and making decisions based upon Christian principles. As one who has shouldered substantial administrative responsibility himself, albeit in the corporate world, Jack prays every day that "God will use George Bush as His instrument, to do the things God wants done."

I think President Bush is doing everything he can to stamp out terrorism. Unfortunately the war in Iraq has crystallized some people's views. Those views don't comport with the Christian way of thinking, and it is causing chaos in the world.
It is increasingly clear in my mind that there is a strong division between the Christian faith and the Muslim world. I am very troubled by that. If we don't somehow get a handle on this, it could lead to continued bloodshed and terrorism. I just hate to think about a world that exists with that going on.

Given this rather bleak worldview, Jack takes tremendous comfort in knowing that someone like George Bush is at the helm. "I shudder to think if we were not led by a man like that. I believe he has sought God's counsel and is carrying out to the best of his ability what he thinks God wants him to do."

That is not to say Jack would vote only for a Christian politician. He carefully analyzes each candidates' actions, looking for a person with principles. The Democratic senator from Connecticut, Joe Lieberman, has attracted Jack's attention. Jack candidly acknowledges he rarely "pulls the Democratic lever," but he is impressed by Lieberman's decision, as a practicing Jew, not to campaign on Saturday, the Jewish Sabbath. In the end, being pragmatic, Jack would consider the nature of the opponent before he ruled out any particular candidate.

If somebody publicly stated, "I am not a Christian. I don't believe in Jesus Christ," I would have difficulty voting for that person. I probably wouldn't vote for that person, unless the person they were running against was even more abominable.

Jack also points out that sometimes there is a grave difference between a politician's words and actions. Simply identifying oneself as a Christian is not sufficient to make one a Christian.

We had a president who claimed to be a Christian. Well, I am not going to question what he says, but I don't believe he really lived the values he professed to believe. There is no way I could, or would, ever vote for him.

Jack worries as he looks ahead to the next presidential election. It is his fervent hope that someone like George Bush, who is a devout Christian, might be elected.

If not, if we don't have that, I think that just further compounds the problems.

After the ritual of baptism was completed and the ushers received the offering, the congregation joined the 300-voice choir and the orchestra in singing a few of the old hymns cherished by so many: "Like a Glorious River," "Peace Like a River," "'Tis So Sweet to Trust in Jesus," and "To God Be the Glory." The music could have warmed the chilliest of hearts. Once the soloist's luxurious rendition of "Call on Jesus" had ended, the faithful were ready to hear the Word. And Dr. Young prayed that he would be a worthy conduit:

> Father, we know that when two or three are gathered in Your name that You're in the middle of them. We know that today that You're in the middle of this worship.... Lord, all of this is put together to give glory and honor to You, so that we might truly worship You not only in spirit but in absolute, genuine truth. Lord, I pray now that You will speak and let me get out of the way so that Thy Word and Thy Word alone might be heard, for we make this prayer in the strong name of Jesus Christ. Amen.[12]

The morning's sermon was entitled, "The Promise of Peace and Deliverance." The text was John 14:27:

> Peace I leave with you; my peace I give to you. I do not give to you as the world gives. Do not let your hearts be troubled, and do not let them be afraid.

"The opposite of peace is fear," Dr. Young proclaimed to his attentive congregation. By way of explanation this eloquent orator directs those gathered to Genesis 3, the story of Adam and Eve. Adam and Eve had been told they could eat anything in the Garden of Eden except the fruit of one tree, which, in defiance of God's will, they tasted anyway. On the evening after they had eaten the forbidden fruit, as usual God came to the garden to see Adam and Eve. Dr. Young, telling the story as if he had personally witnessed the event just yesterday, continues,

> . . .but after they'd eaten of the fruit, Adam and Eve jumped in the bush. And God says, "Adam, Eve where are you? I can't see you." It's not that God didn't know where they were; he wanted *them* to see where they were and to know why they were hiding in the bushes. They said, "We're hiding." He said, "Why are you hiding?" They said, "We're naked." He said, "Who told you were naked?" They said, "We were hiding because you were coming and we are afraid." Now, mark that down: the first result of sin in history is fear.[13]

Preaching like not only his life, but the lives of the thousands who had gathered for worship and the tens of thousands who would watch this service on television in the coming week, depended on it, Dr. Young walked toward the congregation and directed his penetrating gaze at a people made ready to respond and declared, "When we move toward God, we move away from fear."

> . . .and what is the result of that? It is obedience. A lot of people who are Christian think that obedience is not involved in faith. In this book, right here you will never find any place or any time, in any way that doesn't say faith in Jesus Christ, the proof of it is a life that is obedient to Jesus Christ. . . . the proof that you and I have given our heart and life to Jesus Christ and that He is our Savior and our Lord is that we're seeking to be obedient to His Word.[14]

LISA MILNE

Speaking to Me

Certainly there are times with Dr. Young, when he'll preach and I'll say, "Oh, I really needed to hear that." And I will sense that is really God's spirit speaking to me saying something I needed to hear.

Lisa Milne, a warm, bright, a little over "40-something" year-old woman, has been listening to Dr. Young's sermons since he became the pastor of her home church in Columbia, South Carolina, when she was 15 years old. And what she hears now (and has heard for the past three decades from this world-renowned preacher) is a commitment to teaching the Word. First Baptist Church in South Carolina, where she attended until graduating from college, and Second Baptist in Houston, where she has been on staff for the past 28 years, are both Bible-teaching churches. According to Lisa, "That's good."

We believe in the Bible from Genesis to Revelation. We're very clear about what it teaches. We don't pick and choose, although there are times you would like to pick and choose what you are going to believe or act on. Dr. Young generally preaches through a book of the Bible at a time. He doesn't skip chapters or say, "Oh, that's too sensitive right now."

Part of Lisa's responsibility has been to help coordinate Second Baptist's extensive Bible study program. Over half of the church's 43,000 members are enrolled in a Bible study class.

What we seek to do in worship and in Bible study is to say, "This is what God is saying." People love it because they say, "Oh, I get it. I get this book." They are not coming to hear my opinion about society or social issues. They are coming to say, "Help me understand this book." You can go someplace where everybody just sits around and discusses. And if everybody hasn't done homework before they come in, they're just sharing ignorance. I have no tolerance for that. I think it's a waste of time. I would rather hear someone that has really prepared.

As much as Lisa appreciates, even enjoys, the study, she is clear that those who know the Bible are compelled to share its message. This straight-talking, principled woman believes with all her heart that the end result of being a Bible-teaching church is to become a church that offers the "light (the hope) and the salt (the preservative)" to a troubled world. She is concerned that the church in general has not always been effective in that role. As Lisa looks back through the history of the United States, she sees a church that has often been content to remain in the background, rather than entangle itself in the rough places, the cutting edges of society, ministering to broken and lost souls. Lisa is convinced that had the churches stepped forward and done "what they should have been doing," there would have been no need for the government to create a welfare system. She is genuinely saddened that the church has relegated itself to "a stained-glass fortress" of its own creation. Too often she sees those within the church reaching out to their friends or to people like them, while overlooking those in need. She realizes everyone, including her, "just gets comfortable." They enjoy each other's company. Things are going well and they are not all that interested in upsetting their lives with those who may not be quite so healthy. Unfortunately, "we forget the church is a hospital, a place for needy people. That is what we're supposed to be all about."

Meanwhile those people outside the church see no way to penetrate the daunting ecclesial "fortress." She observes that in her parents' generation "almost everyone sensed themselves a Christian" or felt connected to a church in some way. Society has changed and this no longer seems to be true, compounding the difficulty of getting inside.

One of the ways in which Second Baptist has sought to reach out is through its Single Parent Ministry. Lisa's professional responsibilities included administering this ministry, which she feels reflects the way the church should work. For one week each summer Second Baptist supports a single-parent family vacation. This past summer the group went to a dude ranch in Bandera, Texas. In the past they have visited places like Colorado and Disney World. Since many single-parent families must focus much of their effort on survival, they may have limited resources left for building memories. The vacations are an opportunity to do just that. Second Gear is a car-repair ministry for single parents, many of whom are women with little or no expertise in this area. Church members who are car mechanics volunteer their services on weeknights and weekends to do car repairs for the cost of the parts, nothing more. There are also a number of Bible study classes particularly for single parents, which in addition to their study time, provide parents with a vital support network. Though these may be small things, Lisa believes in the end, the small things can make a big difference.

The bottom line for Lisa is that there must be a place for all people within the church. That is what the Christian faith demands, nothing more and nothing less. But finding a place for all people does not mean toying with the scripture, the Word of God, to make it fit individual needs or the needs of a particular community. Lisa maintains that the divisions currently facing the church stem from the efforts of certain groups of Christians to interpret the scriptures in ways that suit their specific needs.

The divisions come about when we're not willing to be obedient to the truth of scripture, when I want to adjust it to what fits me. I can't judge for anybody else how they're to be, but I can certainly say, "Here's what scripture teaches. This is what God clearly teaches is the best way to live." When I choose to live outside of that, I can rationalize, change, make everything try to fit into what I want it to be, but I am not choosing God's way. I am choosing Lisa's way and trying to make God adjust to that. That is always going to lead to disunity.

Division and disunity have wounded the church. The only way Lisa sees for the wound to begin healing is for the sinners to repent and follow "God's way."

It comes back to being really willing to go God's way: to be repentant, to be open. So many groups have dug in their heels, homosexuals would just be one example, and said, "This is who I am. This is my lifestyle, so I am going to make my theology fit who I am and the rest of the church has to accept this with me." From their perspective, if there's going to be unity, I have to make the move; and I'm not willing. I don't think I'm God and I can say, "Okay, maybe God was wrong there, let me change what He wrote."

I don't think there is animosity towards the individual, but towards the sin, yes. I think the heterosexuals would be very open to that group coming back and saying, "You're right. This is a bent that I have, just like some in this church are bent this way or that way, but I am going to do my best to live by the laws God has given." In rare cases I have seen it happen.

When transformation does take place, Lisa is unwavering in her belief that it is due to the power of prayer. The sole avenue toward a changed heart and a right relation with God is prayer. Lisa does not need to be persuaded of the power of prayer; she has witnessed it many times. When she was a child, her father, a military pilot, was in a fatal plane crash, only he did not die. Thus at the age of six, Lisa, along with the rest of her family, became unequivocally convinced that God had intervened in a miraculous way in the lives of the Milne family. More recently a fellow staff member at Second Baptist was diagnosed with liver cancer and given six months to live. Six or seven years later, there is no trace of cancer in this faithful man's body.

But Lisa is not naïve. She knows "there is no magic formula." There have been others for whom she prayed vigilantly, and she watched them die. As a young girl she recalls praying for a dear cousin with leukemia. When the little girl died, Lisa was frustrated and angry. She had prayed that God's will be done. She remembers telling God that never again would she pray for His will; from now on she would tell God what *she* wanted to happen. "I still feel that way sometimes," Lisa admits. "I don't really want what God wants. I want God to want what I want."

As an adult, she finds she can never do enough praying. Praying helps her to "keep her life on track" and to focus on the things God wants from her. Although it is never easy, Lisa sets time aside each day—usually in the early morning before the day gets too busy—to spend in prayer.

It's something I always work at, but if I really work at hearing from God and talking with Him, then I feel more focused all that day.

She always reads the Bible during her prayer time, sometimes a book at a time. Other times Lisa goes back and forth between the Old and New Testaments. It varies. She may read a devotional book before spending time in prayer. Lisa often records her thoughts in a journal. ("I am probably a little ADD [attention deficit disorder], and if I don't have something to focus me, I am kind of thinking of other things.")

Lisa seldom hears God's voice speaking to her in the course of her devotionals. She finds that God speaks to her "through His Word." By the time she was a teenager, she was well-versed in the Bible. She was an intelligent, curious child and she had grown up in the church, hearing the stories.

Looking back, she goes so far as to describe herself as "pretty arrogant." But gradually she became aware of the Bible as God's living Word and that "God wants to say something to me through this." So now her prayer is always that God would show her, as she reads, what she needs to know today.

It's amazing that I can read the same thing I once thought I'd mastered and continue to see fresh and challenging things.

When Lisa joined the staff at Second Baptist in 1978, the church was so small her responsibilities included overseeing high school, college, and singles ministries. Not much time passed before the church grew to the point where she could focus solely on high school ministry, her first love, which she did for almost seven years. In her capacity as Director of High School Ministries, and in the years that followed, Lisa has had ample opportunity to observe the process of spiritual formation in the church's young people.

She has been fascinated to observe that when she talks with the children who are 10 years old and younger, they are absolutely certain when responding to doctrinal and theological questions. Problems that doctoral students might struggle with for hours are completely clear to these percipient children. However, when Lisa encounters these same children as 16- or 17-year-olds ("I've been living here long enough to do that"), issues that made so much sense to them when they were younger no longer seem as obvious. Lisa attributes this shift to humanity's "bent toward rationalization." By the time they are teenagers, these young Christians have begun trying to figure out "what works for them," not always remembering where God belongs, and thus their thinking gets clouded.

Though she has been the Program Coordinator at Second Baptist for the past 21 years, much of Lisa's time and energy is still focused on the youth and families of the growing congregation. Just recently she became directly involved with the high school students again. Thus in the course of nearly three decades in the field, Lisa has developed a well-defined vision of a Christian home. Citing a book called *Soul Searching* by Christian Smith with Melinda Lundquist Denton,[15] she argues that parental involvement in a child's Christian education is key. Too often church is viewed as a place where parents drop their kids for a few hours each week rather than as a community where the family engages together on the faith journey. Experience has demonstrated to Lisa time and time again that parents are the most influential force in a young person's theological development. Thus the program at Second Baptist seeks to nurture the creation of a Christian home.

As she imagines what the Christian home might look like, this playful, albeit childless, woman glows.

It would be fun. There would be life. There wouldn't be a heaviness, but there would just be a reality of Christ in that home, that overriding concept of who we are as a family and a recognition of our relationship with God. Definitely there would be prayer at mealtimes. There would be times of sitting around discussing the Bible and what God says, devotional times, prayer at bedtime. The mom and dad are committed to each other. The kids see a healthy, loving relationship. It's a real relationship. Sometimes Christian families think they should never argue in front of their children. Well, that's not realistic. You don't live with somebody and not have an argument. For children to just be so confident that my mom and dad love each other, and they love us, and we're important to them, and my football game tonight is more important than my mom's social club. You've got a lot of schools where there are all kinds of problems, but there are no parents in the stands. Your presence at your kids' things says to them that they are a priority.

Though Lisa realistically acknowledges that some families do not have the option, she believes it is "awesome" if the mother can afford not to work. Regardless she counsels parents to make sure they have their priorities straight. Perhaps "downsizing" a bit might give the family more freedom. Raising children is not only a priority, it is a privilege. "Those 18 years go by in a hurry. You just don't have a lot of time to shape and mold who they are going to become."

This strong commitment to family has without a doubt been shaped by Lisa's own happy childhood. Since her father was in the military, the Milnes—Lisa, her three younger brothers, and her mom and dad—traveled some when she was a child. After his accident the Milnes returned to South Carolina. Lisa's mother was raised in the Baptist Church, and her father in the Lutheran Church. When the two were married her dad joined the Baptist Church and that is where the Milne children grew up.

Though her father had always been a religious man, after his accident—which left him 80-percent disabled—his personal relationship with God came to life.

From that point forward our family's real focus was recognizing that every day was precious. We had a family where love was expressed without hesitation and without regrets. We just loved each other and lived each day fully. It was a wonderful way to grow up. Mom often took us on picnics and swimming in the summer. She made every day an adventure. Our entire family enjoyed taking our boat to the lake, skiing until it was dark, and then having a picnic in the boat or on an island. We all worked together to get the household chores done so we could have fun.

When Lisa was eight years old she recognized that she "was a sinner" and that she "needed a personal relationship with Christ." After conversations with her parents and her pastor, she made her decision. Her family was very involved in the church, and she delighted in knowing myriad Bible stories.

She was particularly fond of the stories about the life of Jesus and counted Moses, David, and Peter as her other favorites.

At that age I had a very foundational concept of Christianity; I knew that when I died I would go to heaven. I didn't really understand how a daily relationship with Christ worked.

When Lisa was 12 God spoke to her—the only time in her life.

I really felt God saying, "Lisa, I have something I want you to do, if you're willing for me to use your life." I remember thinking, "I am just a little child." But I knew what God wanted me to do. I talked with the pastor and filled out a card that said, "Surrender to full-time Christian service." I didn't know what in the world that meant. All these people talked about me being a missionary. And I thought, "Oh, no, I didn't want to live in another country. I was very thankful to be an American."

After long conversations with her very wise parents, Lisa realized God was asking her to say yes to whatever might come her way, once she was grown up. Three years later Dr. Young became the pastor of First Baptist Church and began to focus the congregation on children and youth ministry. It was under Dr. Young's guidance that Lisa came to understand that God is "not somewhere far away." She developed a daily relationship with the Lord and experienced the ways in which "the Bible could really speak to me." During the summers she worked at the church as a youth assistant until graduating from college, with a major in Sociology and Spanish. It was a few months later that her pastor and mentor began to look toward the Lone Star State.

When Dr. Young moved to Second Baptist in 1978 he brought six people, including Lisa, with him from South Carolina. At the time the Houston congregation was small. According to Lisa, "The records said about 400 attended, but a Korean church was part of that 400. So probably it was much less than that really attending Second at the time." For Lisa the decision to leave South Carolina was a difficult one. Her family and friends were in South Carolina. The church was vibrant and exciting. In the end, she made her decision based upon the realization that there were "more people in Houston to reach for Christ than there were in all of South Carolina." She told God she would go with Dr. Young unless God closed a door.

It wasn't until I started driving to Texas that I knew I made the right decision. I just had that affirmation: you're exactly where you're supposed to be.

For the first 7 years Lisa did high school ministry and for the last 21 years she has been Second Baptist's Program Coordinator. As the church has grown, her job has changed. But she likes to say she is responsible for "all the people-related things." As membership nears 45,000, she thinks of her work with the Second Baptist community as helping to manage a "big town."

Though Lisa dedicated herself to Christian service those many years ago, she has never felt called to the ordained ministry. "I am very, very comfortable with where I am. I feel no limitations because I am a female."

According to the polity of the Southern Baptist Convention of which Second Baptist is a member, each church decides for itself whether or not it will ordain women. Second Baptist has chosen not to ordain women. Its decision is in large part biblically based. Lisa points to biblical references[16] where the pastor is referred to as "the husband of one wife. That is a little hard for a woman." On the other hand, Lisa has never felt that her influence and leadership skills have been restrained by her gender.

I am on the executive staff and many, many of the pastors answer to me. So as far as administrative leadership within a church, there are very few women in America that have as influential a role as I have. The way I look at it, I have total freedom to use the gifts God has given me under Dr. Young's authority. If I have a problem with authority, it's usually not just a person's authority, but God Himself.

The freedom Lisa feels to use her God-given gifts is a sentiment reflected generally in the work of this ambitious congregation. Second Baptist recognizes that it has been blessed with myriad resources. Gifted leadership like Dr. Young and Lisa Milne are only the beginning. Thus, when faced with human need of astronomical proportion, as the Houston community was in the summer of 2005 in the aftermath of Hurricane Katrina, Second Baptist earnestly embraced the task of mobilizing the faithful.

When it became clear people were coming to Houston, the mayor called Dr. Young and said, "Could the faith community mobilize to help us?" Dr. Young said, "Tell us what you want and we'll take care of it." Initially it was the Astrodome. Then they gave the faith community the George R. Browne Convention Center. We took that huge shelter. People were bussed in. We covered food, shelter, serving, everything. We brought in cots and all that kind of stuff.

He's a great leader. Having been in the city as long as he has, Dr. Young pulled together every group, including evangelicals, Buddhists, Unitarians, Hindus, Muslims, Methodists—the whole spectrum of Houston.

Over Labor Day weekend, somewhere in the neighborhood of 46,000 people went through this basic training everybody had to have to be able to serve. And then on Monday, Dr. Young called all pastors and said, "This is how we're organizing." And so, for instance, the first week he put the Baptists, the Muslims, and maybe the Catholics together. Week two it was, for example, the Methodists, the Unitarians, and the Hindus. Each week had radically different groups that worked together. Then he asked all these folks to pledge what their denomination was going to give.

Our church pledged a million dollars; I know we gave well over two. The Muslim group had their million in within a week. All these groups gave and everybody worked together. It was an amazing thing. Twenty-four hours a day, seven days a week. We totally ran our shelter, and we got everybody placed in housing and all taken care of within a three-to-four week period. Roughly 3,000 volunteers a day (sometimes more than that), about 1,000 a shift at three eight-hour shifts.

For some congregations the financial obstacles accompanying this sort of obligation might prove overwhelming. This was not the case at Second Baptist. Unlike many religious groups that resort to rummage sales, chicken dinners, and car washes to bolster their sagging budgets, Second Baptist, whose annual budget is over $46,000,000, "doesn't really do fund-raising." The church has a worship service once a year where members are asked to make a financial commitment for the coming year. Although people are encouraged to tithe their income, it is a personal choice between the individual and God.

So our deal is really the blessed to be a blessing. With what you've been blessed, what would God have you to do? Personally I love to see how much I can give. [Money] is one of those big areas where we figure out if we are going to be obedient to God, or not.

Having been intimately involved with the work of the church, whether in Bible study or car repairs, organizing emergency shelter or attending worship, Lisa is troubled by the way in which the church is often portrayed in the secular media. When she looks at her own experience, much of the reporting belies the truth. She objects to the sarcastic humor and the caricature of the "typical" preacher whose personal life does not square with his sermons. She has observed a similar disconnect between personal experience and secular society in her work with students and their families at Second Baptist.

She recently spoke with a family whose elementary-age child was enrolled in a secular private school. The child's class was planning to visit a Buddhist temple, and the concerned parents approached Lisa to discuss their uneasiness. Lisa is a well-educated, level-headed woman. She has traveled, and even lived, overseas. She appreciates the importance of providing children with a variety of cultural experiences and recognizes that the Buddhist field trip was part of a world-history curriculum. Her objection stems from her assumption that a comparable trip to Second Baptist would not be acceptable.

I guarantee you that school would have a fit if you asked them to bring the student body to Second Baptist. In our society we feel like we need to be nice to everything else, other than evangelical Christianity. There is a huge prejudice against anything that looks like evangelical Christianity today.

She cites another situation in a public school district where a number of Second Baptist children attend. That district had disallowed any mention of Christmas, Christmas carols, or the story of Christ's birth at Christmastime. Lisa had spoken at length with families who were offended by this policy. After meeting with lawyers and administrators, the district officials realized that Christmas was, in fact, about the birth of Christ and although teachers do not have to teach exclusively about that sacred event, neither can they prohibit the discussion of this fact.

In yet another case, she encountered a Second Baptist family whose first-grader was afraid to go to school. After a good deal of discussion it became clear that the six-year-old boy had been telling Bible stories on the playground and somehow found himself in the middle of an altercation that landed him in the principal's office. Being six he did not fully understand the notion of the principal's office and had convinced himself that if he were to continue to share stories of Jesus, which he loved to tell, he would be sent to jail.

Lisa, a genuine woman of God, finds these, and the numerous other stories, to be filled with unnecessary hurt. And although her intellectual and analytical gifts are extremely sophisticated, she cannot quite understand the reason to cause such pain. She delights in the possibility of a church visit from the private school, of explaining the meaning of Christmas, and of a six-year-old eager to tell Bible stories. And on a more personal level, she relishes every opportunity to share her own faith, which she does openly.

I am not hesitant about that because I think anything you love—I love football; I am going to talk about football. You're not going to be with me very long that I don't eventually talk about that.

Lisa concedes that although she loves the traditional hymns like "Holy, Holy, Holy" and "Amazing Grace," and the "bigness" of the choir, she has never been very accomplished musically. Her mother tried hard when Lisa was young. She arranged piano lessons for her daughter, but "it just didn't help, because I was going to be a football player." Lisa still loves football; the Green Bay Packers is her team of choice. And she has made peace with the reality that in the realm of music she is "just a fan." So she talks football more than music, but when it comes to her faith, she is not a spectator. This woman knows how to, and wants to, talk about God.

Obviously I love the Lord. I love our church. Eventually that's going to come out in the conversation. I don't feel I have to maneuver the discussion. And I don't have a set plan I want to take somebody through. Sometimes there are programs you learn. I certainly learned a lot of them growing up. But through the years I have learned to relax. I just love to talk to people, to hear where they are, and to really talk to them about what life could be like. And that's probably my favorite thing to do because I like meeting people.

Lisa is obviously a principled person, unequivocally committed to her Christian faith. She has set high standards for herself, and it is these same standards by which she measures others. When she votes she concentrates on leadership skills and moral values, but she does not require that those for whom she votes be Christian.

I'm unlike some who would only vote for a Christian, or for somebody who was evangelical. I would not make my decisions exclusively on that basis. I don't believe that you legislate Christianity.

That said, Lisa is reassured to know that President George Bush is often at prayer during the difficult times facing the U.S. Government. And she supports his efforts with her prayers.

I believe he is a man of faith and a man that seeks that right guidance. I don't think that that says he always makes the right decisions. But I do pray for him. I would certainly seek to encourage him in those areas in those directions.

In the future, regardless of who holds the office, Lisa will continue to pray for the president of the United States. She will pray that "they seek God, His leadership and His direction, and the direction of wise people around them." She will pray for a person whose moral values permeate every corner of a well-lived life, someone who holds himself or herself to a standard not unlike the one Lisa has chosen as her own.

I can't say, "God, you just stay over here, and I'll see you on Sunday; let me take care of Monday through Saturday." That doesn't work for me. The way I define my growing or maturing with the Lord is by being obedient to the things He tells me. That's sort of a one-word definition, obedience.

5

Somewhere in the Silence: Park Slope United Methodist Church, Brooklyn, New York

On October 31, 2005, the Judicial Council of The United Methodist Church[1] voted to overturn a ruling by Bishop Charlene Kammerer. Kammerer, whose election as bishop by representatives within the church empowers her to oversee 1,209 churches in eastern Virginia, had placed Rev. Edward Johnson on unpaid leave following his decision to deny a man membership to South Hill United Methodist Church because the man refused to renounce his homosexuality as sin. The Judicial Council rejected Kammerer's action and ordered Rev. Johnson to be reinstated immediately. Reactions to this ruling were immediate and emotional.

The Reconciling Committee[2] of Park Slope United Methodist Church (PSUMC) in Brooklyn, New York, gathered for its monthly meeting three weeks after the Judicial Council decision was announced. Kathy Dickinson was hosting the meeting. Her lovely townhouse facing Prospect Park is reminiscent of the elegance that now eludes many residents of the Brooklyn neighborhood. She made meatballs, a few others brought cookies. The Roches' *Zero Church* CD played in the background:

> Call me, Jeremiah, and I'll show you great and mighty things you have never seen before.
>
> (Jeremiah 33:3)

Cushion-covered couches beckoned, but some of the nine-member committee chose the floor. The talk was of completing college applications, a parishioner who had taken a fall, and Thanksgiving holiday plans including pleas for a weekend dog sitter. In many respects this was an unremarkable gathering, although the group did include two high school seniors who had not just willingly but eagerly joined their mothers for the meeting. The only male in the room was the pastor. About 35 minutes after the designated gathering time, the committee's chairperson, Dorothee Benz (or simply Benz to those who know), opened the meeting. She asked those assembled to share their response to the Judicial Council's ruling. Each person spoke in turn. Benz began.

I've been fighting for 21 years. I've always kept my membership [in The United Methodist Church]. It's my church. I've always said [to the others], "you leave." But this is shocking. My gut response was, "screw it." Sort of like the veneer of respectability was torn away and there stands naked bigotry. I find it hard in moments like that to find God, to know that God's there, somewhere in the silence.

"It took the wind out of me," Park Slope's pastor, Rev. Herbert Miller, explained.

It's really the straw that breaks the camel's back, makes me want to throw up my hands and run. But I have spent my life working for the unity of the church, of the wider Christian body. It is not those who are well who need a physician, but the sick. The church is ill. I will keep trying to bring healing.

The lay leader of the church, Judy Fram, went next.

I didn't even know this was an issue. Who are these people? I stay a Methodist for the same reason that I stay an American even when Bush is my president. It's a dysfunctional family, but it's still my family. This [decision] has made me more stubborn. Maybe it will finally galvanize people who are on the fence.

People talked and listened. They shared stories about growing up Methodist in Mississippi and leaving ("or getting kicked out") and about walking away from Catholicism and heading toward Park Slope United Methodist Church. Some proudly, even defiantly declared themselves "lifelong United Methodists," while others said they had not joined *the* United Methodist Church—they had joined *Park Slope* United Methodist Church, "and there is a difference."

Though their meetings usually begin with devotions, no one had been assigned to lead the group in prayer and reflection that evening. Benz had just completed a move into a new apartment with her partner Carol (one of the mothers in the two mother-daughter duos present) and apologized for not being as well prepared as she had hoped for this meeting. After everyone had offered their reactions, Benz asked if anyone had a scripture to share.

Judy went to her bag, got out her Bible, flipped through, and found this passage:

> I am astonished that you are so quickly deserting the one who called you in the grace of Christ and are turning to a different gospel—not that there is another gospel, but there are some who are confusing you and want to pervert the gospel of Christ. But even if we or an angel from heaven should proclaim to you a gospel contrary to what we proclaimed to you, let that one be accursed! As we have said before, so now I repeat, if anyone proclaims to you a gospel contrary to what you received, let that one be accursed!

> (Galatians 1:6–9)

This scripture had "jumped out" at Judy as she thumbed through the Bible. To her, it spoke "of another gospel, a gospel of the institutional church instead of the Gospel of Christ and his radically inclusive love."

Congregants of Park Slope UMC have been committed to the Reconciling Congregation Movement since its inception. In other words, they are committed to reversing what they believe are "unjust" policies adopted by the ecclesial leadership prohibiting the full inclusion of gay and lesbian people in The United Methodist Church, policies they believe are derived from a misguided commitment to "a gospel of the church" rather than "the Gospel of Christ." In the year and a half preceding the Judicial Council decision, Park Slope had already established itself as an effective leader in the Reconciling Congregation Movement of the New York Annual Conference.[3]

The group moved from the living-room floor to the dining-room table. Benz laid out a four-point agenda, and the work officially began. As Benz reported on a conference-wide gathering of Reconciling United Methodists, the committee members became animated. The timing of this meeting, on the heels of the controversial Judicial Council decision, was both poignant and fortuitous. The focus of the conference-wide meeting was a discussion calling for another larger conference-wide meeting, which would in turn call for a special General Conference[4] in order to reverse the Judicial Council ruling. "There would," Benz declared, "be no more business as usual."

"More meetings?!" People were incredulous. "Meetings to call for more meetings? What about that is not business as usual?" Those around the dining-room table were not satisfied with this course of action. They demanded an explanation.

Benz was weary. Her assessment of the conference-level gathering had been that it "was very good. Not so much for some brilliant plan that came out of it—modest, good plans did, but nothing to wow you. But some good folks showed up..." and she felt like people really wanted to do something. Now Benz was sitting here—surrounded by people who love her, who admire her, who pray with her—eating meatballs and trying to muster the energy within herself, within her own soul, to continue to work for a more inclusive

United Methodist Church. She was looking for ways to realize a vision of a United Methodist Church where gay and lesbian men and women could be husbands and wives, ordained pastors, and cherished lay members—a United Methodist Church that would embrace her with the same devotion, compassion, and commitment she bestowed upon her beloved church.

DOROTHEE BENZ

The Right Time

Dorothee Benz was raised in the church, the First United Methodist Church in Montclair, New Jersey. In 1968, when Benz was three, she and her parents moved to the United States from Ludwigshafen, Germany. They were Lutheran. Uninspired by the minister at Montclair's local Lutheran church, Benz's parents explored their options and chose The United Methodist Church. So, Benz, this passionately committed United Methodist, smiles a little and admits that her lifelong membership in and dedication to The United Methodist Church is an "accident of the Lutheran church not having the right minister at the right moment." Her membership may be an accident, but her commitment is clearly a choice.

As a child, Sundays for Benz meant dressing up ("dresses but no hats, white gloves, or patent leather shoes") and going to church, a little hard to imagine since jeans and a T-shirt seem to be her preferred uniform these days. The day's dinnertime ritual was an intellectual inquiry into the theological foundations of the morning's sermon. Her father professes a devout, unswerving Christian faith, while her mother's faith is more of a give-and-take, at times even a struggle. As a self-assured teenager, her mother's moments of doubt were perplexing to Benz. In retrospect she is quite clear about her mother's confusion.

Benz considers her father to be one of the most faithful people she knows. Still, what Benz appreciates about her father is that he does not wear his faith on his sleeve. She muses that his colleagues may not even be aware he is a Christian, though his active involvement with groups like Habitat for Humanity stems directly from this lifelong, deeply rooted religious commitment. Benz describes her father as a "do it but don't brag about it kind of guy." She admires this.

Thanks to her father, she has no trouble reconciling science and religion, or faith and intellect. Growing up she saw the two as naturally compatible in the man who is her father, a scientist with a Ph.D. in chemistry and a man of unshakable Christian faith. Given her own proclivities toward intellectual analysis, an unexamined or blind faith is simply not an option for Benz. She claims her father's rather rare ability to balance scientific inquiry and religious belief as a "lucky inheritance."

In many respects the notion of inheritance seems fitting. Benz has faith. It is a gift she has been given. Her faith is a part of her like her thick, brown hair is a part of her. Sometimes longer, sometimes shorter, sometimes all neatly in place, most times not, it is what she was born with and what will cover her head until she dies. As a child, she had "always had that young intense earnestness of how do you live this?" By the time she was 13 her aspirations to become a mathematician had been overshadowed by thoughts of entering the ministry.

In 1983 Benz went to Harvard. Having been raised in a loving, but fairly restricted German Christian environment, Benz chose a different route in college. Her college years were characterized by critical thinking, political activism, and an active social life. She was certainly "aware of the world" in high school; she read the *New York Times*.

I knew I didn't like Ronald Reagan, but the college years kind of brought the house down. I came out as a lesbian, pretty much as soon as I got [to Harvard], which was wonderful and glorious. I am lucky that I never had a day in my life when I felt like being queer was a sin or was wrong, or was bad or shameful, or something that I should hide. I never had a day in my life when I felt that. I don't know exactly why.

By all accounts Benz "had a wonderful, chaotic freshman year." Then in May 1984, the General Conference of The United Methodist Church voted to amend its Book of Discipline to read, "No self-avowed practicing homosexual" shall be ordained or appointed in The United Methodist Church.[5] The 1984 decision effectively banned gay Christians from serving The United Methodist Church as ordained clergy. A gloriously gay committed Christian, Benz would not be permitted to pastor a church in the denomination in which she had been raised.

I was a young, religious, lefty, zealous radical from a privileged background. And all of a sudden I come up against the reality that I can't do this. Had I come from a less-privileged circumstance, I wouldn't have been so shocked. It was my first really huge slap in the face on this issue, and it made me so angry. It enraged me. I spent the next ten years angry.

But she stayed in the church. (Benz maintained her membership in the First United Methodist Church in Montclair. Though it is not required, she contributed $100 annually, so as not to be a burden to her home church.) She poured her angry energy into writing "angry polemics." She engaged in a sophisticated exchange of letters with one of the editors at *Sojourners Magazine* (a publication committed to integrating spiritual renewal and social justice) and published a long treatise entitled "The Failure of Protestant Churches to Confront the Sin of Homophobia" in *Religious Socialism*, a publication of the Religion and Socialism Commission of the Democratic Socialists of America. She wrote with intense passion, and her work was well received among those she considered colleagues and kindred spirits. But Benz saw no changes in ecclesial policy nor any spiritual conversions as the result of her efforts.

I can hold my own in a theological argument, but in the end, I'm not sure that's what matters. There are very few people I've ever met in my life who are actually capable of changing their mind based on an argument.

Her father happened to be one of the few.

He confronted me at dinner one night in the summer of 1984, after a weekend when my new lover had visited. Of course, she was introduced only as a friend from school. I asked, "What did you think of Suzanne?" (something the adult in me with 20-plus years of hindsight recognizes was asking for trouble). My father responded, "The weekend was entirely too lesbian for me." I forget exactly what followed: some anger and expressions of shock on his part. No denial on mine. I was devastated. I was afraid of him; I thought he might hit me, though he had never lifted a hand to me in my life. Later in the evening he said we should talk the next night when he got home from work. The next 24 hours were among the scariest of my life.

That next night, when we sat down, he began, "What you told me last night was a shock, and I've realized that the most shocking thing about it is that, compared to the fact that you're my daughter, nothing else matters." He had done in just over a day what many parents take years or decades to do. From there, the conversation went to a series of sincere questions from him: "How do you know you're gay? Why do you have to tell other people?" et cetera. They were questions asked nonrhetorically, without malice, genuinely searching for the answers. At the end of a long conversation, he said, "I can't say that I accept it, but I tolerate it."

Two nights later, at dinner, he brought the topic up again, and said, "The other night I said I tolerate, but don't accept it. That is wrong. I accept it." He added something to the effect that it's tough enough dealing with others' nonacceptance, it would be wrong for a parent to add to that kind of rejection. He's been pretty consistently supportive from that day on.

One year after she graduated from college this highly educated, highly energetic young woman moved to Brooklyn. She started looking "on and off" for a church. As a successful career trade unionist and doctoral candidate in political science, Benz had a full life, at times a bit too full. She had no time for religion, but for Benz faith was not the kind of thing one has time for. Having faith, like living each day, is simply something she does. So she looked for a community, a place of sanctuary to share with others. She visited a church whose congregation consisted of eight octogenarians, but she had a ways to go before she reached 80. She visited another that had good Left politics. But she already had good Left politics; she needed theology. She tried the Riverside Church in Manhattan: good theology, great politics, but too big. She looked around for awhile, "but nothing really took." Looking back, she is convinced, "That was about me and not about anything else. I wasn't ready. The time was not right."

As she wandered in a wilderness of religious institutions, her Christian commitment never wavered. She maintained "a not very disciplined prayer life." But she needed community. Eventually she concluded Park Slope UMC was the right "congregation." She uses the term congregation, not church, intentionally, since it is the people with whom she sought connection. There was no miracle, no parting of the waters.

It was a sporadic choice over a couple of months. I kept saying, "Oh, I have to go to church this week," like "oh, I have to go to a meeting."

The church was nearby. So her uncomplicated decision to attend Park Slope UMC was nothing more, but it was also nothing less. She attended off and on ("more off than on") for over ten years. Then in the spring of 2003 Benz had a romantic disaster. She was "profoundly crushed" and really in need of community in her life. Very matter of factly, she explains, "Something said to me this is the moment that you need to get your ass back to that church. And I did. It felt right and I stayed." In the first or second week, she saw Carol singing in the choir. (Awkward conversation at coffee hour followed, but it was many months before Benz could overcome her shyness and figure out how to initiate a courtship.) In the winter of 2004, convinced that she had "been there long enough," she decided to join "the place." Benz contacted her father and asked him to transfer her membership from First United Methodist Church in Montclair, New Jersey, to Park Slope United Methodist Church in Brooklyn, New York.

Benz has never been one to sit on the sidelines; congregational involvement followed rapidly.

I don't know what possessed the Nominating Committee to ask me to chair the Reconciling Committee. Maybe they thought, "Hey, here's a new gay person who hasn't done anything." But for whatever reason they asked me to co-chair the Reconciling Committee. I thought, "I can't do this. I just finished a dissertation. I am as burned out as a human being can be. I have a full-time job. I am teaching on Sunday afternoons, and I just got into a relationship. And if I do anything I want to spend time with Carol—hello." But I didn't say the magic word "no," and they took the nonresponse as a yes.

She had hedged only briefly. Creating a truly inclusive UMC had been a defining issue for Benz for over 20 years. Here was an opportunity to use her impressive organizing skills to work for change within the institution she loved. She concluded the Nominating Committee's request was maybe a "right time with the right kind of talent" kind of thing; as opposed to, for example, Park Slope's Wednesday evening Taizé service, which Benz loves but does not participate in much because she needs to be home in the evenings to care for her blind dog, Thurgood, and she adds, "anyway I can't sing."

But there have been a few dark nights when, singer or not, church was where she wanted to be. And church was where she went. It is another right time with the right kind of talent kind of thing, and Benz is wise enough to know that sometimes the talent comes from somewhere else.

It was mid-February, but this particular Wednesday evening was mild. The pastor and some church members were lingering on the sidewalk. After a few minutes they went inside. The Taizé service began.

The sanctuary is mostly dark-red wood. A mangerlike construction, made out of live—now dried—greens rests right inside the door. Hundreds upon hundreds of small, seemingly handmade, white stars hang in the entryway and throughout the worship space. The stars are in no particular pattern, or perhaps more accurately, no obvious pattern. Candles illumine the altar and the rest of the sanctuary. The lights are low. The floor slopes toward the front, drawing people in.

The 30 or so who had gathered came quietly into the silent, candlelit sanctuary. Carol and Benz slipped into the service a few minutes after it had begun. Benz had just found out she lost her job. She was, by her own admission, feeling beaten down.

The service was smooth, somehow graceful. The participants found the transition, from the noisy world outside to the stillness of the sanctuary, surprisingly easy. They had done this before, many times. For those who are here each week, the service connects them to a solid spiritual rhythm. For those who come in times of need, they find what they expect. Words, music, and silence slowly, beautifully, simply fill the room. And then there is the pain. Ten minutes of silence is long enough to hear the hurts and sorrows of anyone's heart. Over and over voices joined together, praying and singing:

Within our darkest night
You kindle the fire that never dies away,
never dies away.

As they sit together in the dark, the song echoes from the souls of those who have lost jobs, those who worry about health, family, relationships, and finances, those who struggle to free themselves from poverty or drug abuse, those who long for a world without war.

Within our darkest night
You kindle the fire that never dies away,
never dies away.

Everything is not okay, but God is here and God will stay here, even when things are not okay, even if you cannot sing.

When her graduate school classmates found out Benz is a person of faith, their jaws dropped.

Look, I am a visibly identified, butch lesbian, fairly foul mouthed—use the word "fuck" like a comma—hard-core socialist, left-wing trade unionist. It doesn't fit people's idea of what a Christian is, which is too bad.

It is too bad, she clarifies, that those characteristics are not part of the typical Christian stereotype.

Her co-workers knew that Benz is a Christian. Although she, like her father, does not "wear her religion on her sleeve," she also laughingly concedes, she is not her father. Outgoing and lively, she readily admitted (she is amused by her word choice) to co-workers that she had to leave the office to get to a 7:00 church meeting. As her work with the Reconciling Committee grew more interesting and she became more involved in efforts to change official UMC policy on homosexuality, she shared her struggles and her successes with friends at work. For Benz this witness was a significant aspect of reconciling ministry.

She is honest about her faith, her politics, and her sexuality, and she is sure about the connections.

To me there is nothing sinful or wrong or shameful about being gay or having gay sex. It is unambiguously clear to me that this relationship with Carol was meant to be. This was ordained by God. God is in this relationship. My faith is completely wrapped up in this relationship. It is so intertwined, it is so clearly, so profoundly divine, that nobody could tell me there is something sinful here.

The connection between her faith and her politics is equally apparent. Benz has always been struck by the Beatitudes and the parable of the sheep and the goats. (Matthew 25: 31–46) In the latter she recalls one point when

Jesus says, "You did good, and when you helped somebody else you helped me out." But she is not ready to leave it there, for this Christian socialist the goats must be dealt with as well.

The other side of the parable is when Jesus says, "You didn't help, you really fucked up." That speaks about the obligation; it's not just that it's a good thing to do. No, you have to do it. That side of it means more to me. I always felt that as tantamount to a call for socialism. I have a really hard time reading the Gospel without reading it as a mandate for social and economic equality, which as a political scientist I translate into a political system.

My politics is informed by my faith. And I've always had Leftist politics as long as I've had politics, and they have always seemed to be absolutely self-apparent in the Gospel. No one had to tell me that. It just seemed right—completely, transparently, unavoidably true. It's really hard for me to wrap my head around right-wing Christians, not so much interestingly enough on the hot button issues of the day—abortion, gay rights, right to die, and stuff like that, although I can't really wrap my head around that either—but on issues of poverty and class and one's obligation to be part of a community that cares for the poor; it's completely impossible. You can't crack open the New Testament and not run into that on at least every other page. I don't see how the religious Right has managed to make a political juggernaut out of everything else but that, and the religious Left (which isn't even a real term, which is sad in and of itself) has not managed to slap them down and say, "Hello, it's easier for a camel to pass through the eye of a needle than for a rich man to enter into the kingdom of God." That stuff has always been apparent to me.

Benz finds confirmation of her social, political, and economic beliefs in the life and work of Jesus.

You can't ignore Jesus' constant challenge to social norms. I've said this so many times I feel like a broken record. Jesus' ministry—the way that he eats with tax collectors and lepers, talks to women, and tells stories about Samaritans—does every kind of thing that breaks social lines of exclusion from his time, transgresses social norms very deliberately. How can that not translate into what we are called to do as Christians?

Not surprisingly, Benz has some specific ideas about the ways in which Christians respond to this call. For her the scriptural mandate to feed the hungry and house the homeless involves more than spending a night volunteering in a shelter or a passing out a turkey sandwich at the soup kitchen.

Those are worthy things that I wish I did. But all of them on some level make me crazy. The problem is people are hungry. People are homeless. They can't afford homes. We live in an unjust society that denies basic human needs. True faithfulness to the Gospel requires us to fight that system, to truly fight, not just hand a sandwich or blanket to somebody for a night, but to roll up our sleeves and march on city hall or on Washington, do that work. That doesn't, by the way, mean that I don't think the other work is important. If the world were full of people like me and nobody was handing out the sandwiches and the blankets, it would be devastating. But there's an unavoidable piece of the Gospel. It's not just about helping the less fortunate and creating a more just society for them. It's about the recognition of the poor as people of sacred worth and the rich as somewhat morally handicapped. And that's the real hard piece, to walk out there on the street corner and look at that guy who's sitting there, kind of crazy, and see Jesus Christ in him, see him as someone just as worthy as yourself. I'm not any better at that than anyone else.

Benz rejects the idea that working together to respond to the biblical challenge to feed the hungry and clothe the naked could provide a way to bridge the growing divide between the religious Right and the religious Left, particularly evident around the issue of homosexuality. "Justice delayed is justice denied," she quotes William E. Gladstone. An astute political strategist, Benz realizes this type of partnership may make sense as an institutional strategy, just not hers.

I get it politically, pragmatically, there is always going to be conflict within the church. I know I'm right, but that one over there thinks she's right, too. Shit, I don't want to destroy the church in the process of trying to fight this out, so let's just sidestep it. I get that from a pragmatic point—a pragmatic Christian desiring to do the work of God in the world. I just can't bide it as an answer, not only because I'm on the other side of the exclusive line on that particular issue, but because I don't think unity is a value that trumps all others. That can be a cover for "let's not change anything."

But if "argument" is not an effective means for "changing peoples' minds," and Benz persists in her belief that change is necessary *and* possible, how does that change happen? Now in her early 40s, Benz finds hope, inspiration, and resolve in her faith. Arguments may not be able to change people, but God can.

I persist in acting as though people change their minds. I'd go mad and sink into unbearable despair if I didn't. I think that people sometimes change their hearts and that helps them change their minds. It is a trite overgeneralization, but there is something to it.

Take the case of straight people warming up to the idea that homosexuality isn't a sin, or a "lifestyle," that God made some of us queer, that God celebrates the diversity of human sexuality, and we should, too. The most successful way to get people there is to put gay people in their path, gay people that they know and like—like their kids. The love for a child (or sibling, friend, or co-worker, et cetera) works on the heart to transform socially inherited prejudice.

I see God as an active presence in the world. I believe that God acts on the human heart. Luckily, the human heart is the site of God's most intense miracles. I don't need to judge whether other people are capable of being open to God's radical love and justice. I just act as though they are. Being a person of faith impacts my strategies: I believe all people are redeemable. I believe that nonviolent resistance, as pioneered by Gandhi and practiced by King, is the single best, most powerful political and spiritual tool available to the oppressed and the poor. The power of nonviolent resistance is that it acts upon the heart of the perpetrator; by responding in love instead of violence, it transforms the person using it into a mirror in which the perpetrator cannot help but see his violence. That alone makes it possible to bring about transformation and lasting peace.

Benz has no trouble articulating her thoughts and beliefs; indeed she relishes the opportunity to engage in spirited conversation. She approaches her relationship with God in a similar fashion. Benz knows a "noninterventionist God (for lack of a more elegant term)." She believes in a God who answers prayers, just not like a waiter taking an order; to her that would make absolutely no sense.

When we open ourselves to God, through prayer and meditation (among other things—like mountain climbing, for instance), prayers are answered through divine presence and transformation . . . not always or usually even in a recognizable form to us.

But Benz nurtures an active prayer life. She uses the example of flying, which she does not like. She is afraid of flying, yet when she gets on a plane Benz tries very hard not to pray, "God please don't let this plane crash," because she knows that is a prayer that cannot be answered. So the prayer that she prays is, "God, please let me be able to deal with, give me the strength, the grace, the calmness, to deal with whatever happens with this plane."

I hate turbulence. The prayers I believe can be answered have to do with the heart and with the head. They don't require some kind of flashy miracle, like tricks in a magic show. So for me the goal of a much more disciplined spiritual practice and prayer life is to get more of that—to really have an active piece of God constantly flowing through me—to tap into that more and more and more.

She finds the *lectio divina*[6] suits her well. She strives to rest in God's presence. Although she easily admits she is not there yet.

To sit down quietly, let alone rest, in God's presence is a feat I have not mastered. But I am convinced it's a learned practice. I just have to work at it, and I can get there. I recognize the way to get somewhere is practice it every day.

She recalls a phrase somewhere in Paul's writings about praying without ceasing. Benz used to ask,

What the hell does that mean? How can you do that? Now, I get that. It's not like taking time to stop and pray; it's your every step, your every word, every step of your day is done in this incredible conscious shared presence of your human self and something—and God.

Connecting her human self to that something, to God, has been difficult lately, being out of work, struggling with United Methodist polity. . . . But she is okay with that. One of the things that she has gleaned from her pastor, Herb Miller—a man whose spiritual guidance has been significant for Benz— is that faith is also a relationship, a right time in the right place kind of thing.

There are fallow periods and you just keep going. Other people, your faith community—those with whom you share sanctuary—will carry you, and you have faith that your faith will be strengthened.

HERB MILLER

Starting to Calm Down

It was my first church, my first church service. I remember getting to Lakeville United Methodist Church, a rural Connecticut congregation with less than 50 members, and thinking, "What do I do now?"
  Seminary had just torn me up. The critical scholarship, I had no problem with, but I didn't know how to make sense of it, how to integrate it, how to live faithfully with all of it. None of that integration happened, so I felt like, "there's no way I can pastor a church." I didn't know how to hold it together myself; I certainly couldn't hold it together for other people, preach weekly sermons. I didn't have anything to say.

Herb Miller needed and wanted to say something, but he was not quite sure what. He graduated from Yale Divinity School unsettled and uncertain. Herb had chosen Yale because it was the alma mater of his mentor, Hal Vink (that the seminary was ecumenical and close to his home in Valley Stream, Long Island, were sort of the icing on the cake). What Herb saw when he looked at the church changed once Hal Vink became part of the equation. Herb had always been a churchgoer; everyone in his family was. But it was not until he began listening to this young, radical pastor that he started making the connection: worshipping God meant a reshaping, or a reordering, of society. Vink's radical preaching flowed from a radical gospel, which demanded nothing less than radical action.

Vink took Herb, and the other high school youth, to the farms on eastern Long Island. The pastor needed the farmworkers to do a little "preaching" to these teenagers. A white, middle-class, suburban boy, Herb was less than oblivious to the realities of his Christian brothers and sisters. He had not forgotten the farmworkers; he was never aware of their existence. Herb was stunned to discover that the workers were paid in alcohol. The teenagers accompanied their pastor to the farms on a number of occasions. The young people enthusiastically gathered clothes and household items for the farmworkers. Then the youth group worked together to raise some money for the people who so generously shared their precious stories of faith and hardship—but mostly faith—with these hungry young believers. Sitting in his parsonage 30 years later, Herb reflects, "It was all new to me—the problem, yes, but also how faith affects action."

His insights had been reinforced by youth-run summer church-camp experiences, where Rev. Vink and other progressive pastors kept social issues—like apartheid in South Africa, economic inequality, and sexual inclusivity—in front of the young people. The pastors insisted that the youth assume leadership positions at all events, honing organizing, networking, and public-speaking skills. These spirited and spirit-filled pastors continued to make connections between faith and action, and at least one young person was listening. "It just blew my mind away. I had never heard any of that."

Herb's plan, and Herb's family's plan, had always been that he would go to medical school. He was a self-avowed science whiz. He had won all sorts of science awards. He started college (West Virginia Wesleyan College) as a Psychology major. His studies were demanding, but he found time to become involved in the local United Methodist church. The whole time he was in college, he smiles, "people kept telling me that I should consider ministry, but I kept resisting it; I'm not sure why. I guess I was holding out for some other idea about what I should be doing." But the church was an important part of his life. Herb became deeply enmeshed in a Christian education program working with rural churches in West Virginia. People continued to tell him, "you're good at this, you should do this." For a long time he mostly felt entangled, caught by everybody else's clarity. He found himself looking for the way out. After college, the only thing Herb could say for sure was that he was not certain he belonged in the ministry.

"I figured I could waver some more by going to school some more." So he enrolled at Yale Divinity School. Medical school was no longer on the horizon. Halfway through college Herb had completely lost interest in science. He had graduated with a double major in Psychology and Christian Education.

Seminary was a good experience. Herb encountered professors who were active in the lives of local churches. His teachers chose to live in the poorest areas of New Haven, in solidarity with the marginalized, those lifted up in the Gospel whose theology these accomplished scholars practiced as well as taught. At Yale, Herb witnessed real faith. "It was attached. And I felt more and more nudged. Yes, this *is* what I should be doing." While in seminary, Herb worked as a chaplain at South Central Community College and as an intern at the Darien United Methodist Church. The divinity school's community focus on a strong and innovative worship life provided a challenging, yet safe, place for him to stretch his soul. Nonetheless, after graduation, in the midst of the ordination process of The United Methodist Church, doubts surrounded him. He still was not sure where he was supposed to be.

So Herb got out his backpack and went to Europe.

Oddly enough in the course of that trip Taizé came to mind. It sounds flaky, but I didn't know anything about it. I had heard the community mentioned once in a liturgy class, a document about the Eucharist. So, I began asking people I met about Taizé. I found someone who knew what it was, and then a ticket seller at a train station told me where it was. I got on a train to Paris and then to Taizé.

It's hard to say how it changed my life, but it taught me how to pray. Before I went there, I didn't have a prayer life. I didn't know what prayer was, other than asking for things when I needed them. I had no concept of less verbal forms of prayer.

Although prayer is the cornerstone of the Taizé community, Herb describes the community's commitment to this spiritual discipline as having a "light touch." The faithful gather three times a day for singing and then silence. Herb has a beautiful voice, which he is not shy about sharing. It was the silence that he found arduous.

At first I didn't know what to do; I had never spent time in silence. I could go through my laundry list: oh, God, I need help with this or with that—but their whole thing [at Taizé] is to just be with God, to rest with God, and a sense of oneness and being will just naturally well up within you. Whatever was going on within me started to calm down. I saw a lot of other possibilities. I committed myself to silence at that point. Ultimately it has been a savior in my ministry, constantly calming—which is not the goal, but definitely a by-product. It has kept me out of a lot of trouble. Watching the way the brothers interacted full of grace is a wonderful model. It firmed up my calling.

Herb was wearing old blue jeans and beat-up sneakers and a surprisingly lightweight jacket given it was February in Brooklyn. As his parishioners neared the church that evening, they could see him standing on the corner. Rather than go inside, they stood with him for a few minutes enjoying the mild winter evening. Relaxed conversation, and gentle teasing—what was Herb doing on the corner? Looking for more people to fill the pews?—mingled with the noises of the city.

Without consulting a watch, his or anyone else's, Herb remarked, "I guess we should get started." Those entering the sanctuary found everything—the bulletins, the candles, the music—had been prepared for them. Herb's handsome bass voice guided the congregation through the simple, truth-telling songs. Someone played the piano. A teenager played her flute. And the congregation joined in song.

> To you, oh God, I lift up my soul. . .
> To you, oh God, I lift up my soul. . .
> To you, oh God, I lift up my soul. . .

If one is able to lift up his soul to God, God must be present. Some souls may need to be lifted out of some desolate places; but on this evening, those gathered are finding, through song and through silence, the strength to lift up their souls. And they are lifting them up to God.

When the service ended everyone sat still for a few minutes. Herb went over and turned on a CD of soft instrumental music. People sat for a few minutes more and then quietly began to leave. The bulletin directed people to gather outside or downstairs if they wished to socialize. Most chose outside.

At Taizé Herb did not find a place with all the answers, but rather a place to share the questions. During Bible study he began to focus on what the text meant for him. He started to look inward. He was introduced to a life of prayer, a place of rhythm. The churches where he had worked during seminary were riddled with committees, polity, and infighting. At Taizé, he saw there were other ways. He saw a place where the church was authentically the church. There were no power games. Everything was done with immense grace and gentleness. Herb experienced genuine community and found the personal resources to enter into the ministry. He still did not know how to do it—maybe his hesitation and hope would never be completely untangled—but he knew what he had to do.

Herb was the pastor of Lakeville United Methodist Church for four years. Looking back, he is sure that God blessed his ministry in that rural Connecticut community. Attendance increased and the Sunday School grew. But he felt isolated and after three and a half years he did not know what else to do. So he asked his district superintendent for a different appointment.[7] Later that year Pastor Herb Miller was sent to Diamond Hill United Methodist Church in Cos Cob, Connecticut. The congregation was tiny—20, maybe 30 people. Herb served that church faithfully for 14 years. Unlike so many of his colleagues, Herb learned *not* to equate his value as a pastor or the efficacy of his ministry with membership numbers, annual budgets, and building capacity. He grew to love the smallness of the church, to appreciate its intimacy. There was less politicking and fewer power struggles; people took care of one another.

This little, working-class congregation struggled financially, in the shadow of Greenwich—one of the wealthiest communities in the United States. The church is located on Route 1, a main commercial thoroughfare. There were lots of people in and out of the building who needed help finding food, clothes, and housing—basic needs really, not unlike the needs Jesus spent time satisfying. The congregation, under Herb's guidance, engaged in a fair amount of hands-on work with the poor.

Their most time-consuming project ("really it was all-consuming") was an affordable housing program, which Herb inherited from his predecessor. The church acquired houses in the neighborhood, many of which were in abhorrent shape. The church rented the houses in an effort to provide affordable housing in the neighborhood. Renting the houses also helped bolster a sagging church budget. By default, Herb ended up as director of the small housing project. He fondly remembers some of his more worldly tasks as pastor at Diamond Hill UMC, like dealing with people's stopped-up toilets and settling tenant disputes. Herb was often called when the weather turned cold. Some of the tenants, especially those not used to Connecticut winters, had difficulty adjusting to the cold. The houses were always set to 69°F, but each year the church found it necessary to install thermometers to demonstrate to the tenants that their homes were adequately heated.

[The work in the housing project] was a drag, but it was good. It forced me to look beyond the theoretical implications of poverty, to build relationships with people who were struggling. It changed the way I looked at things.

In the beginning none of the tenants attended Diamond Hill United Methodist Church, but over time they all ended up going to the church. Of course this was wonderful, and tricky, since the church was still their landlord. In 2002, two years before Herb was to leave Diamond Hill, the church secured a half-million-dollar grant to renovate the homes completely. The congregation was pleased with this development, but having the much-needed work done created its own complications. All 14 residents were displaced. Work that was projected to take 6 months stretched into 18. A number of families from the congregation opened their homes to the folks who needed to be relocated. Herb marveled at the tremendous hospitality of this small congregation.

On the one hand, it was hell; on the other hand, it was great. People really lived up to the challenge.

Herb is deeply committed to living the Gospel message of housing the homeless, clothing the naked, and feeding the hungry; but only if these tasks emerge from a spiritual place—from study, prayer, and praise. He introduced his congregation to the prayer and music he had learned at Taizé. He established a Bible study (his "favorite thing") not worrying so much about places and dates, but urging the participants to consider where the text is taking them in their lives and how it is calling each person to transformation. The sessions were always grounded in biblical scholarship, but Herb would not permit those gathered to hide behind "the facts" in lieu of dealing with some tough personal questions.

Herb was searching for a way to use Bible study to move people even more passionately, more intensely, into lives of service when he came across the work of the Church of the Saviour in Washington, D.C. It just "kept popping up in books," he muses. Following his heart, Herb went to Washington and was amazed at what he saw. The church was running a home for men and women with AIDS, a retirement home for the elderly poor, and services for people who were homeless, to name only a few of the ministries. The more he saw, the more questions he had.

How did this happen? The programs were done with such grace, not just plopping food on the plate, but done with such integrity. It made me dig deeper to find out what was going on.

He learned that the Church of the Saviour is firmly committed to contemplation *and* action. For years the church had been nurturing its Servant Leadership School. Members routinely read Dietrich Bonhoeffer and Karl Barth.

They found themselves inspired by the talking and the discussion, but they weren't "fully there" somehow. Then they stumbled across this melding of contemplation and action. The model is not "I go to a prayer group" or "I go to a Bible study" and then "I go to a group that's doing social activism." It's all one small group, and it's all organized around a common call. Members agree to participate in daily disciplines, which include study, prayer, and mission. Members of Church of the Saviour focus on the area in which they feel called, rather than trying to satiate this diffuse sense of "I should be doing something" and dabbling in a lot of things, but in the end doing nothing of great consequence. Having joined a small accountability group, members become accountable to a life of service.

This organizing principle, the blending of action and contemplation, resonated with Herb. He began exploring this model of ministry with his congregation in Cos Cob. He recognized that it would be a long process; the church in Washington searched for 20 years before it found this path.

Herb was granted a month-long sabbatical. He volunteered in the Church of the Saviour's long-term health-care facility for homeless men. He participated in the worship life of the community. Church of the Saviour gave voice to what Herb had already realized about measurements and ministry. He found affirmation in that prophetic community's assertion that "faithfulness disappears with size." Church of the Saviour includes a number of small "churches," with approximately 20 members in each. He was intrigued by what he saw: accountability groups, led by volunteer lay people, had become minichurches. Making use of the church-run bookstore, Potter's House, members are constantly studying. Each group meets and worships in one of the mission spaces (such as the shelter or the retirement home) so additional administrative costs are minimal at best. Members commit to sharing 10 percent of their income with the poor.

Having seen it at work, Herb began trying to replicate the model in his church in Cos Cob. He started an accountability group. The leaders of the Church of the Saviour advised him to begin with a group organized around a call, since commitment to the call, not to the group, should be the starting point. But Herb was not sure the people of Diamond Hill UMC were ready to articulate a particular call, so he brought together a group (with the intention of disbanding after a year) to help his congregants to discern their calls. As a result, a couple of people worked much more intentionally with the local soup kitchen. They began a project to gather leftover baked goods from local stores twice a week. Had Herb stayed longer, the accountability groups organized around a common call might have emerged. But after 14 years, Herb received a call of his own—from the district superintendent. Herb would be moving on.

Herb had not been planning to leave Cos Cob. On the contrary, he was looking forward to implementing the small-church mission model. This time he did not ask to move. This time the district superintendent called him, offered him an appointment at a church in Park Slope (a middle-class Brooklyn neighborhood), and said, "You have 24 hours to decide."

I thought they [the district superintendent and the bishop] were going to leave me alone. The call took me completely by surprise. I didn't know how to process it. I woke up the next day, and I couldn't call. I needed one more day to pray on it. I woke up the next day, saying, "I don't know why, but I need to do this." And I was getting ready to call Jane [the district superintendent] and the phone rang. It was a woman from the church in Park Slope who wanted to tell me how glad she was I was coming. I guess I'd been appointed before I made my decision. Well, it wasn't my decision anyway.

Throughout his tenure at Diamond Hill UMC the demographics had changed. The congregation had gotten younger, but the numbers did not change much. Then again for Herb church growth was something spiritual, not numerical.

Park Slope UMC has a long and powerful history of radical Christianity—former Nicaraguan president Daniel Ortega preached to the PSUMC faithful in the early 1980s; the congregation is a founding member of the Brooklyn Ecumenical Cooperatives, a grassroots initiative that sponsored one of the area's largest nonprofit housing projects, and the church has embraced a policy that states no one can be married in the church until all can be married in the church.

When asked how he feels about the politics of fellow United Methodists President George W. Bush, Vice President Dick Cheney, and Senator Hillary Clinton, Herb bridles a bit:

I am severely disappointed and embarrassed by all of them. I think charges should be brought against Bush and Cheney within the church; they have been the source of such extensive human suffering and have destabilized the world. Bush once turned down a meeting with UM Bishops. I think they should keep knocking at his door.

When he arrived at PSUMC, Herb found a surprising mix of openness and resistance to his commitment to a spiritual life that embodied action *and* prayer. As he became acquainted with his congregants, Herb sensed that people were hungry to develop their prayer life and build community.

That's why meetings go on for three and half hours. People feel, "I want to give myself to something." I'm just hoping I have the wherewithall to take them to the next step.

Feeling settled in his new parish took time. There was naturally some tension as these very empowered lay people adjusted to their new pastor and their new pastor figured out how to deal with a congregation more than eight times the size of his previous church. Nonetheless worship attendance was well over 100 during that first summer, a record high. And the parishioners told him and anyone else who would listen that they were delighted with Herb. The only specific "complaint" he recalls was that the trustees wanted him to attend their meetings more regularly. Since he has no expertise in this area, he has suggested they may need to function without him. He also butted heads a bit with the Social Action Committee members over the nature of their work. Herb wanted the committee to dig a bit more deeply into one area rather than simply being "wet towels" on many different hot spots. For their part some on the committee wanted him to be more explicitly political in his preaching, though he is not inclined to move in that direction. He is clearly interested in and keeps abreast of a wide range of political issues. And although his sympathies lie with the Left, he does not consider himself to be a political analyst.

Herb's life is completely interwoven with his faith. His faith affects all of his decisions, including political ones. At the same time, his faith does not square neatly with the platform of any political party.

I give my loyalty to Christ before giving it to the Democratic Party. I understand that Christ's ways are radical, countercultural, and often not intuitive or even "reasonable." It is an alternate Way. I can't expect those outside the faith to ever fully live into those ideals, but I can work towards constantly nudging in that direction. In speaking to fellow Democrats I try not to lean in so far as to fall in.

That said, Herb believes the church has an unequivocal prophetic role. And he does not shy away from using his voice as a religious leader.

My preaching isn't political in the sense of tearing apart and offering clear political analysis. I don't always have the time or expertise to offer well thought-out specific resolutions to various crises. I do, however, raise issues of concern that need our attention and work. I try to give general Gospel principles that pertain to a variety of political issues. I sound the constant call for each of us to work towards justice, reminding the congregation of our obligations. I try to inspire people to address the issues that call out to them.

Sometimes specificity narrows the message too much. As a preacher, I can sound a prophetic voice on one issue at a time, or I can call and encourage a hundred and twenty people to be prophetic voices in their many spheres of concern and give them the language of faith to move forward. The trajectory of my ministry is to get people to own their issues, being faithful with the small, encouraging and allowing them to raise their passionate issues in a number of ways in the life of the church—sharing the pulpit, after-church forums, information dissemination, tabling during coffee hour, letter-writing campaigns. I acknowledge that often we are each called to be a source of healing to different pains in the world. We each have different concerns and issues that break our hearts, enrage us, are the constant irritation under our skin, that demand our attention. If we each pay attention to those issues that call out to us with faithfulness and integrity, together we will be a source of healing. We will each heal a different part of the body and make us all whole.

The program he is most excited about is a class he is offering now for the fourth time: "Inward Journey, Outward Journey." This is a seven-week course for 12 congregants drawing on the work of the Church of the Saviour and K. Killian Noe's book *Finding Our Way Home*.[8] Herb is hoping to move Park Slope in the direction of this mission-/call-based model of ministry. He hopes to take members of his congregation to visit the Church of the Saviour, but has not done it yet.

It takes time. Call doesn't come overnight. What I am struggling with now is how to keep people moving, but not forcing it.

JUDY FRAM

A Chocolate Thing

The voice I am hearing is not one I recognize. I don't recognize this person who has such a faith...a faith that permeates my life. I don't know how I got here. It sort of crept up very slowly.

It is not that there have been periods of unbelief, or even moments of doubt, in Judy Fram's life; but neither has there been a lightening bolt, a flash when some bright light revealed everything, filled her with the spirit of God, and her life was somehow different. If one were to try and find a visual image for her spiritual sojourns, the labyrinth seems right: many twists and turns and no straight path, but no dead ends either.[9]

For me it was more like baby steps: someone whispering, "go over there, now go over here." I fell into things, a very slow, deepening process.

Judy is a sophisticated, sagaciously spiritual woman. For the last couple of years, she has participated in a lay-speaking ministry class.[10] She was already an enthusiastic member of Park Slope UMC when she began attending the classes. She participated regularly in worship and was involved in many aspects of church life. But the opportunity to testify about the transformative power of prayer or to witness to one's personal relationship with Jesus was rare among the Park Slope UMC faithful.

It wasn't really cool to say you were a Christian. So the lay-speaking classes became kind of my outlet for those months. Even if the other participants were theologically or politically very different from me, I just felt so comfortable, being very bold about my faith. For some of the people, it was just like every breath, their faith was always there for them. It was a privilege for me to be with them.

Judy recalled the give-and-take before, during, and after the classes. Though the group did not really talk about politics, the topic of the Bible and the church's stance on homosexuality did come up. Judy rejected the equation of homosexuality with sin. She urged the full inclusion of all people in the life of The United Methodist Church. These positions were unacceptable morally and unsupportable biblically for a number of her classmates. Those were difficult discussions. They happened more in the second year than the first, once the group had built a certain level of trust.

I found out I was not alone. We were in the minority, but I was not alone. I don't think anybody's mind was changed, but everybody was respectful and everybody listened to everybody else. There were two youth in the class, and, for all I know, maybe that was the first time they heard anything that was remotely different from what they were brought up with. I have no idea what they were thinking.

Judy has registered for a third year of classes. And the culture at PSUMC has started to shift. Judy is moved and inspired by the way in which Pastor Herb Miller's spirituality permeates everything he does. In Herb, she encounters a gifted communicator and a progressive theologian who is also comfortable in the realm of very traditional language. He confidently proclaims his faith. After attending Herb's "Inward Journey, Outward Journey" class, Judy has felt things stirring, opening up within the congregation.

I guess the classes made me bolder. I just started saying things about my faith. I really stopped caring about what other people thought.

Still the conversations at PSUMC are never easy, seldom simple, and rarely brief. According to Judy, many of the congregants at Park Slope UMC are either unchurched or they are coming in with religious backgrounds that were "not fun." Many suffer from what she calls "Bible abuse." People have difficulty negotiating theological minefields, often raising questions like, "If I accept this [scripture], what will it mean for those I care about? Is this against women or is this against gay people?" The congregation openly struggles with these questions, and Herb is right there with them. Judy has found Herb's focus on the Bible very helpful. He preaches from the Bible, often embracing rather than avoiding the difficult texts.

For a lot of people [in the congregation] the Bible is not a place they would go for inspiration. They would go to another book. They would go to Martin Luther King, Mother Teresa, or Gandhi, not necessarily to the Bible, although I think that's beginning to shift a little bit.

I would like to know the Bible at least as well as my cousin who is a very conservative Christian. If you are biblically literate, you have more chance to dialogue with people who have different opinions. To me it's not enough to write it off and say, "It's a patriarchal book or it's confusing." It is confusing, but I'd still really like to know it a lot better. With Herb's help, other people in the church are now starting to say that, too. Biblical knowledge is there, but being able to call that up is not something we did before. It was kind of like, "Let's just say what we think and not rely on the Bible at all because that gets misinterpreted." But now hopefully people are thinking, "If it's misinterpreted, then let's reinterpret it in a way that makes sense." They don't feel that you just have to reject it because it's been misused. I think people are beginning to be more interested and more open.

Somewhat of a scholar in her own approach to spirituality, Judy relishes books, all kinds of books. She is a voracious reader. Her reading is a significant piece of the foundation of her spirit-filled life. She points to a volume, *What the Bible Really Says about Homosexuality,* by Daniel A. Helminiak, another called *The Secret Life of Bees* by Sue Monk Kidd, and a third entitled *Soul Survivor: How My Faith Survived the Church* by Philip Yancey, which she found provocative, comforting, and soul-stretching. "Revelation," a short story by Flannery O'Connor, truly inspires the authentic search of this dedicated woman.[11]

O'Connor puts it right out there—our self-righteousness and how we tend to rank people, judge people. I love how truthful she is, how descriptive she is, and how her character really does have this amazing revelation. She writes like a kick in the head, and the fact that she writes with a spiritual bent makes me love her even more.

Judy has gotten into the habit of reading *The Upper Room* every night before she goes to sleep. She reads the scripture that accompanies the brief devotional, the devotional meditation itself, and the week's lectionary reading.[12] Judy concludes with a prayer from Carmen Acevedo Butcher's book *Incandescence: 365 Readings with Women Mystics,*[13] poems and prayers by women mystics. She is drawn to this particular prayer book because its language has a different kind of harmony. It moves her mind in another direction.

Sometimes, if the scripture speaks to her, she studies some more. She will get out her *Interpreter's Study Bible*[14] and go through the Bible passage. When there are Old Testament references in a New Testament passage she goes back and looks at those hoping to get a bigger picture. She examines the text at hand from myriad angles—trying to understand the intention of its author and, much more importantly, its message for her right now. On her own, Judy engages in elaborate, sophisticated study of the scriptures and theological literature. Her motive is simple, "I am just so hungry to know."

The written word, however, is not Judy's only source of inspiration.

I walk the park. I walked the park this morning. I was just looking at the trees and noticing that they're all in different stages—some of them already lost their leaves, and for some of them it's going to be a while yet. Like people, for some of them spiritually it's a period of rest. I am always looking around creation and seeing what it might be saying on any given day.

Judy and her husband, Michael, knelt side by side in the front of the sanctuary. It was mid-February. Michael had had a hard week. Though the weather was unseasonably mild, he sought the warmth of the darkened, candlelit sanctuary, the quiet of the Taizé worship. Having settled in the front, the space between the couple and the aleatory array of small, white candles surrounding the altar was empty. This was not the case were either one to direct his or her gaze off to the left, where row upon row of books filled the pews—used books in large, white plastic bags, with labels like Reference, Foreign Language, Domestic Arts, and Children's Books. Judy was very familiar with the categories. She was one of the setup people who had helped sort the donated books. With any luck, the pews will be empty again by Sunday, since Saturday is the annual Park Slope United Methodist Church book sale. This is a "huge fund-raiser" for the church, which generally earns over $8,000 ("at a dollar a book, that's a lot of books") at the event. As PSUMC's lay leader, Judy will certainly support the sale. But right now, she is singing.

> Come and fill our hearts with your peace.
> You alone, O Lord, are holy.
> Come and fill our hearts with your peace.
> Alleluia.

To be able to sing alleluia, alleluia, over and over is to claim that there is something to rejoice about. And the congregation sang. It was not just a half-hearted, going-through-the-motions singing, but singing that swelled the hearts and souls, that warmed even the wood and fueled the flames.

> Come and fill our hearts with your peace.
> You alone, O Lord, are holy.
> Come and fill our hearts with your peace.
> Alleluia.

Participating in the worshipping community of Park Slope UMC has carried Judy along her journey, along the meandering, yet focused path of her labyrinth. Every sermon Herb preaches is a challenge, which she loves.

There were years when I went to church every Sunday to get what I could get out of it for myself. Now it's about getting out of it what I need so I can go out and do something.

When she is able, Judy turns her attention to the people who are homeless in her neighborhood. She gives a little money, buys food, offers clothing, and chats with them on the corner. She participates in the Gay Pride parades and helps staff the Pride table. And she spends time in prayer.

I try to pray for people. I pray at home every night. I have come to see prayer, time with God, as necessary for my going on with God's work and my life. I try to be available for people in need, in church and out.

She is excited that she and the others in the "Inward Journey, Outward Journey" classes have been grappling with questions about call. PSUMC is now fully staffing Tuesday nights at a neighboring church's homeless shelter—part of the pastor's effort to get people to put their faith into action. "Of course," Judy continues, "the congregation did that before, but it was different. Then it was things like marching against the war."

There is still a contingent from Park Slope UMC at every antiwar march. "I support that, but," Judy confesses, "huge marches are not my thing." (She did participate in the PSUMC peace march one evening a month, until it ended.) It is often the same people, but the church always has a presence at political events. Given the congregation's progressive political identity, over the years the question has arisen as to how to be tolerant when faced with others, particularly people of faith, who profess differing views.

Every once in a while there is someone who disagrees who is strong enough to stand up and say, "I disagree." We joke about the fact that my husband and I both voted for Bloomberg [then a Republican mayoral candidate, now the mayor of New York City] then received an e-mail from someone in the church making the assumption that anyone who voted Republican was an idiot. The e-mail came a day after the election, so I didn't feel the need to respond.

Judy's political decisions are without doubt affected by her faith. Her principled yet nuanced thinking is reflected in her choices and actions.

Over the years my choices have been for candidates I believe will represent Jesus' goals for the poor and marginalized, whether they come from that person's faith or not is not an issue. I demand someone of intelligence and integrity, which to me is not the same as perfection or not having anything to regret. I listen to people I respect, watch the news, read the papers, and end up going with some instinct I cannot explain.

I am called not to judge anyone, but I can't help wondering if Bush or Cheney have actually read Jesus' words. I have people in my family who think Bush and Cheney are wonderful leaders. This is a challenge for me, to say the least. I love my family, and I am called to love all God's children. I am pretty sure Jesus knows this is really hard sometimes.

I am an admirer of Al Gore; after the film *An Inconvenient Truth* came out, I wished the timing were such that he was the strong and personable man of the film during the election when he was running. Clinton was a hard act to follow, for both good and bad reasons, but I admire Gore's commitment to this planet and its life as I see it there in that film. Also I think Rudy Giuliani did quite a job in this city and country after 9/11. I will not forget his love of this city and the leadership and comfort he provided to so many.

Judy and a number of PSUMC members volunteer at the shelter on Tuesdays. This recent initiative to get involved in the shelter is more tangible, and perhaps, Judy imagines, a more traditional Christian response to the biblical mandate to put faith into action.

That's always something I think about. I would like there to be fewer differences between us and conservative Christian groups. I mean where we differ, we differ. But we could focus on the same kind of basic needs of the poor, reaching out in faith to people and stuff like that. That's what I would like to see.

There is a bikers' saying Judy loves that goes something like "when you slide into your grave you want to be totally used up." She is attracted to this idea.

I try to think of that from a Christian point of view: do everything you can do. Although I guess I don't think of myself as always [working]. There are needy people crying out on every street corner. I struggle with how much to do and when to rest with God and/or family and friends, and hope I'm not being lazy. I suppose my vision is, I hope God's vision, where people have what they need, love and materially, and are not addicted to what they think they need.

I do a lot of fun things. I don't consider my life to be really serious all the time. I am always reading and stuff. But on Friday nights we go to see a band that we like. We've probably seen them 40 times. They're a family band. They play in a bar. We take my daughter. It's really relaxing.

Judy likes the work of Donald Miller, author of *Blue Like Jazz: Nonreligious Thoughts on Christian Spirituality*. There is a passage in that book that captures her approach to religion and life perfectly. The author recounts a conversation with his friend Penny.

...if you ask me, Don, the Bible is so good with chocolate. I always thought the Bible was more of a salad thing, you know, but it isn't. It is a chocolate thing.[15]

This rare combination of an easygoing, almost playful approach to a highly disciplined spiritual life has not always been Judy's *modus operandi*. It was having her first child that helped her find her way.

For me, parenthood was like a kick in the head. God can reach out to people in many different ways and sort of get somebody to really slow down and understand about surrender and unconditional love. It took becoming a parent for me to be able to learn those things. Other people may be able to learn them without that, but I couldn't. The whole process of giving birth and understanding what surrender is, and trusting. I was always a very busy person. I worked full-time and went to graduate school. I didn't have a lot of downtime in my life, and that was fine. But having a baby taught me to slow down. Surrendering and enjoying my baby's breast-feeding taught me how to enjoy a moment, to understand what peace feels like, and to accept the power in surrender and gifts shared. That was the way God spoke to me.

As her children got older (she has a girl and a boy), Judy decided not to return to her job as a physical therapist, but instead became a lactation consultant and La Leche League volunteer. Though she rarely shares her faith with her clients ("I'm there to serve them and usually they are in crisis anyway"), her work is a concrete manifestation of her faith.

Infants are potentially very vulnerable, and their needs are often forgotten by a culture that separates families and pushes women in so many different directions. Whereever I can help build a good relationship between a mother and her baby, that's where I go.

Often as she works she finds herself praying for those she encounters. Her favorite scripture is a verse from the book of Matthew, "Come to me all you who labor and are heavy laden and I will give you rest" (Matthew 11:28). She prays for all to find rest.

Judy has worked with the same women for a long time, yet the revelation of religious faith—hers and theirs—has been a slow process.

It's certainly not the first thing we knew about each other. I don't talk about it at La Leche League meetings because that's not what they're about. But the other leaders, they know. It's just sort of another piece of who I am.

Now her colleagues are aware of her religious commitment. They knew when she was working on a sermon, eagerly encouraging this first effort; and just as Judy respects her Jewish co-worker's Sabbath on Friday evenings and Saturdays, her co-workers do not schedule clients for Judy on Sundays. As her faith has become more central to her identity, and she has become more intentional in her walk through the labyrinth, she has also become more intentional about the way in which she identifies herself.

I can't remember where I read this, "whatever I am—a spouse, a parent, or a person of a certain ethnic background, or a person who lives in a certain place or who doesn't like certain things and does like other things—what if the most important thing people knew about me was that I was a Christian? What if that wasn't the last thing on the list, what if it was the first thing?" After I read this, I started rethinking myself, shifting. Instead of, I'm this, this, this, and this. It's "I am this," and that's why all these other things matter or happen or whatever.

Unlike many who trace the source of their spiritual journey to family, Judy's beginning is less clear. As a child, Judy was the only one in her family who went to church. From the time she was young her dad dropped her off at church so she could attend worship and Sunday School. Except for Christmas Eve and Easter, she went alone. Possibly her affinity for church had something to do with her grandparents. They are Methodist, and when she visited in the summers, she attended the Methodist church with them. Looking back, she is not really sure how, or why, it all happened; she just remembers wanting to go to church. When she was too old for Sunday School, she became a Sunday School assistant. For a brief period Judy's little sister joined her, and her dad dropped both girls at church on Sunday mornings.

When her family moved from New Jersey to upstate New York, Judy found a Methodist church. She attended Sunday services, sang in the choir, and went to youth group on her own.

Going to church alone was no big deal. My parents never talked about it, but they also never said, "I don't want to take you today." What I remember is that I would ask them to drive me and they'd drive me, until I got my license and then I'd drive myself. It just wasn't an issue. My mom was a nurse, so she often worked on weekends. She made me a confirmation dress, and my family came to my confirmation.

Judy is trying to make sense out of these childhood churchgoing years.

I think what really attracted me, more than the theology which was sort of hazy, was the singing. I loved the singing in worship. The music always drew me in. I don't remember any particular anthems, but I remember what the choir robes looked like. They were blue with gold trim. People in them looked content. I felt somehow wonderful when I wore one and sang for the people. The choir sat separately and faced the congregation. I remember a meditative song, "Lead me, Lord, lead me in thy righteousness."

An 11-circuit medieval labyrinth has "34 turns on the path going into the center. Six of these are semi-right-angle turns, and 28 others are 180-degree U-turns."[16]

During her college years Judy definitely encountered some turns on her path, but she never lost sight of the path. In 1978 Judy started college at Stony Brook University. In her sophomore year she fell in love with a Jewish man. He had said from the outset it was essential for him to be with someone who was Jewish—which Judy was not. Although this man did not attend temple and was not even sure he believed in God, his identity as a Jewish man reached to the core of who he was. It was vital to him, and to his parents, that he raise a Jewish family. Judy tried to understand what it meant for him to "be culturally Jewish." She was in love. She studied about Judaism and carefully considered converting. She was in college and then just out of college. Her friends were either Catholic or Jewish, no Protestants. She was not attending a church. She was not even thinking much about her faith, but for Judy the idea of abandoning Christianity was incomprehensible. Christianity was not a significant part of her daily life. It seemed as if it should not be that important. But Judy could not let it go.

The relationship was just sort of fading away when one of her patients (Judy was by now a successful physical therapist), a nearly blind, elderly, Caribbean woman, said, "That boyfriend you have, he doesn't love you. That one," the prophetic woman continued, pointing to a man standing in the hallway outside of Judy's office, "he's going to love you. He's the one you're going to marry." Twenty-four months later, Judy and Michael, the man standing in the hallway, invited the wise old woman to their wedding. Unfortunately she had returned to Jamaica.

Winding around another turn in the labyrinth, Judy recalls that during their first date she asked Michael about his last name.

By the way, what is your ethnic background? I can't really tell from your name. He said, "I'm Jewish." And my mouth dropped open. I just couldn't believe it. My first thought was, "you did it again."

That year (1983) Judy was training for the New York City Marathon. Michael bought a bike and rode along next to her. She ran and he rode through Brooklyn's Prospect Park. When she needed a longer run she headed out to Coney Island. They had huge talks about religion. They discussed everything—the Lord's Prayer and baptism, his bar mitzvah in an orthodox synagogue, the holidays celebrated all in Hebrew. She just chatted away. It gave her something to think about other than how far she was running.

The couple concluded their religious differences were "not an issue." When they were married, there were two weddings: a Methodist service in the morning, at the church where Judy had attended youth group as a teenager, performed by a Methodist minister who had been born Jewish and converted to Christianity; after sundown there was a Jewish ceremony in a restaurant nearby.

We didn't really feel like we were married until we'd been married twice. We did the whole thing, broke the glass and had the blessings. Michael's uncle stood up with us and read scripture. Our intent was if we had children, we would bring them up understanding their roots in Judaism and Christianity.

When their son was born, they traveled from their home in Brooklyn to upstate New York to have him baptized since they were not affiliated with a church nearby. When it was time for her daughter to be baptized, Judy decided to look for a church closer to home. She had been attending a predominantly African-American congregation, Grace United Methodist Church, around the corner from their Brooklyn apartment. Her husband joked that he was willing to be the only white man in the church, but he was not sure if he could be the only Jewish white man in the church. So Judy looked in the phone book and found Park Slope UMC.

The first Sunday she went to the church, she heard the song, "My Lord, What a Morning!" which she had always loved, and she saw someone she knew from La Leche League. The pastor agreed to baptize her daughter with the stipulation that Judy attend services for awhile first. The next week her husband came with her son, who started Sunday School. They have been at church every Sunday ever since.

As planned, their children have been raised with Jewish and Christian traditions. Judy and Michael host a Passover celebration every year—fondly referred to as the Passover for the marginally Jewish—with five interfaith families. As far as Judy knows, of the five, hers is the only family that maintains any regular religious observance. Most of the rest are culturally Jewish. There are some in the group suffering from church abuse, some ex-Catholics, and some people who were raised knowing they have Jewish heritage, but with little else. These families have celebrated Passover together for six years. They use the whole Haggadah with a mixture of English and Hebrew. The kids participate. Everyone reads, taking turns around the table until they have completed the entire ritual.

At Hanukkah we usually light the candles, but we don't give a gift every day. We used to celebrate Hanukkah with another family, but as the kids got bigger . . . no, it had nothing to do with the kids. We got cats and they're all allergic. They still haven't forgiven me.

The kids seem comfortable with their mixed background. If my daughter meets somebody who's Jewish, she says she's both. But I think she self-identifies as a Christian.

Judy's family spends Christmas with her parents. They attend church on Christmas Eve and open one gift that evening. Near midnight they enjoy shrimp cocktail. When their children were younger, the Fram's went to the early service with a live nativity.

It was inside, a shorter service for children and families, no burning candles. Then we went out to the barn to see the people dressed as the Holy Family, and all the live animals. This was quite special, usually frigid and quiet.

The labyrinth that is Judy's life always seems to draw her back toward the center.

It is October 2006, three weeks before the first anniversary of the Judicial Council's monumental decision regarding Bishop Kammerer's punitive actions against Rev. Edward Johnson. Benz sent out an e-mail to more than 150 Reconciling United Methodists. She is trying to pull together a strategy session to continue efforts toward building an inclusive church. She has not heard back from everyone yet. But still she is sure, somewhere in the silence, God is there.

6

Politics of the Pew: Does Where You Stand Depend on Where You Sit?

Faith is personal. For people of faith no celebration or sorrow exists separate from faith. It is deeply entwined in every story of life and death. Each decision, no matter the scope, is somehow molded by one's faith.

Perhaps it is because faith is so personal that interpreting the political impact of people of faith is so complicated. Following the 2006 midterm election, there is growing evidence that the Republican Party (Grand Old Party—GOP) does not have a monopoly on Christian voters. Although a majority of conservative evangelicals appear to have supported the GOP, the religious Left had considerable impact on ballot initiatives throughout the country and in electoral races on all levels.[1] The recent increase in political activity on the religious Left and the religious Right has renewed interest in age-old questions concerning the relationship between politics and religion and the long-term political and theological viability of using religion as a base for political organization.

Theologian and journalist Diana Butler Bass objects to the current trend that seeks to classify churches as red or blue, either Republican or Democrat. In the course of her research, she has discovered an abundance of purple churches. Bass describes purple as "an ancient Christian symbol" borrowed by the early Christians from the Roman imperial empire to represent the reign of the Christian God.[2] In today's color-conscious society, she argues purple still has social, economic, and political significance.

> For Christians, purple is more than a blending of political extremes. Purple is about power that comes through loving service, laying down one's life for others, and following Jesus' path.[3]

Though Bass does not advocate a church that turns its back on society, she is concerned about an overly politicized church. She concludes, "Christians should not be a voting block. Christians should be disciples of Jesus."[4]

This is not to say there are not clear connections between one's faith and one's politics, but rather that Christians need to be clear about their priorities. At no point should politics or politicians be permitted to set the agenda for a people of faith.

Though it is unwise to make generalizations based upon less than 20 profiles, it is definitely illustrated in the preceding chapters that the political decisions, of anyone for whom faith is important, will be affected by his or her faith commitment. It is, however, of critical importance to add that in every case discussed in this book, faith leads and politics follows. In other words, faith sets the course, and other activities, including political decisions, ensue.

Those profiled are similar in significant ways. They are white, middle-class or upper-class Christians. They are highly educated, professional people. The only obvious difference among the various individuals is geographic. This does not seem sufficient to account for the radically divergent, even con-flicting beliefs these Christians profess. They study, and preach from, the very same texts. They remember and sing the very same songs. And yet some are genuinely tortured by the presence of the others, in whose lives they see the work of Satan.

The American Protestant community is a community divided. Divisions within the faith are nothing new. They date back to the beginning of the church itself. The United Methodist, the Presbyterian, and the Southern Baptist denominations each were birthed from division. Nonetheless, know-ing that separation has been commonplace since the church's inception brings little comfort to those who find themselves mired in the struggles of today.

At first glance it may appear that the only theological connection these individuals have with their counterparts is a sentimental soft spot for that beloved old hymn "Amazing Grace." Though none of these dedicated Christi-ans had the opportunity to meet those whose lives fill the chapters other than their own, were they to interact, some conversations might be difficult, frus-trating, even sacrilegious, while others might be surprising, heartbreaking, and perhaps inspirational.

In the end, prayer seemed to be the place they all wanted to go. Without exception, when questioned about their faith journeys, people wanted to talk about prayer. It was not always an easy discussion, but it was essential. For Debra, prayer has helped focus her grief, "I struggle with my faith over the loss of my son...I find it difficult to pray. And I try real hard at it...I do have a constant dialogue with God all the time...I hope that's prayer." Herb remembers a time when he, too, was working at prayer, "At first I didn't know what to do; I had never spent time in silence. I could go through my laundry list: oh, God, I need help with this or with that—but their whole thing [at Taizé] is to just be with God. . ."

Each of the people who have shared their stories aspires to a life connected with God through prayer. And though they endeavor to "bathe" every part of their faith-filled lives in prayer, they approach their Creator in different ways. Some seek silence either alone or in community. Others are "pray-out-loud-kind of pray-ers." Some embrace a routine of daily quiet time in a particular place, at a particular hour. Others yearn for every breath and every step to be an embodiment of prayer. For most prayer is a profoundly personal conversation with God. Some seem relaxed in their interactions, almost on a first-name-basis with their Maker. Like Stephanye, who easily admits, "I don't pray pretty prayers. It's just like, 'Okay, God, I'm in the car and I've got my cigarette lit. What are we going to talk about on the way to work today?'" Others talk about being quiet in order to hear. Tony reminds his daughters to sit still if they are having trouble hearing God's voice; perhaps they are "not being quiet enough."

Some talk about a feeling in their hearts, and others talk about God's will revealed through His Word. The ways in which they experience God's response to their prayers is at once breathtaking and heartbreaking. God has answered some of their prayers. Jack recalls a phone call from his son, and Ginny witnessed God's healing touch on more than one occasion. Others have felt God's distance and been filled with confusion, frustration, and at times even anger. Lisa knows there is "no magic formula," but still wishes she and God always wanted the same things. Debra has little tolerance for those who are privy to the healing power of prayer since she knows too many who are not. No one seems so sure why God responds in the ways God does, but each one of these people feels compelled to communicate, to keep the conversation going—making sure God hears their voice and trying to discern God's message for them.

So personal prayer is an area where the conversation among those profiled might be engaging and nuanced, but not particularly charged or contentious. That is until the content of some of the prayers was made explicit. Almost every person interviewed claims to pray for the leadership of the United States. Many mention President George W. Bush by name. However, some are praying President Bush will continue to have the strength to do God's work, while others are praying that the president's heart will be transformed so he might repent from his misguided ways. These are all people committed to a life of prayer. People of faith—of the same faith—are praying prayers to the same God, and yet their petitions could not be more different.

Jack, who approves of Bush's efforts to eradicate terrorism, prays every day that "God will use George Bush as His instrument, to do the things God wants done." Lisa is reassured to know that President George Bush is often at prayer during the difficult times facing the U.S. Government. She also supports his efforts with her own prayers. On the other hand, Judy, like the president and the vice president, a United Methodist, takes issue with her country's leadership, "I am called not to judge anyone, but I can't help wondering if Bush or Cheney have actually read Jesus' words." Herb, Judy's pastor, believes The United Methodist Church should take ecclesial action on behalf of its membership, "I think charges should be brought against Bush and Cheney within the church; they have been the source of such extensive human suffering and have destabilized the world."

Jack, Lisa, Judy, Herb, and all the others are committed Christians. And as such they have trouble understanding how this vast dissimilitude is possible. The beliefs and interpretations that are diametrically opposed to theirs make no sense to them. The question (how can *they* believe *that*?) is almost palpable.

Fred and Jack, both members of Second Baptist, are confident their perspective is true to the Christian faith. Fred explains, "The Republican Party is far from perfect, but it is the party that values life and fosters...family values. How can a Christian vote Democratic with a party that leans so far left, allows abortion to happen—the killing of millions of babies—and promotes policies which harm the family?" He sees no justification for a Christian to vote for a Democrat, "Recently I asked a close friend whose opinion I value, 'How can someone who says they're a strong Christian vote Democratic?' And they said, 'There's a difference. There are people who really read the Bible and those that just claim they read the Bible." Jack concurs, "When I look at the Bible and read what it says, there is no way I can get to where they are... How can you be a Christian and believe in abortion, not have a problem with homosexuality, commit adultery, and all those sort of things? How do you do that and still say you believe in Jesus Christ and his saving grace?"

Judy and Benz, both members of Park Slope United Methodist Church, see things differently. As if she were responding directly to Jack's honest inquiry, Benz explains, "To me there is nothing sinful or wrong or shameful about being gay or having gay sex. It is unambiguously clear to me that this relationship with Carol was meant to be. This was ordained by God. God is in this relationship. My faith is completely wrapped up in this relationship. It is so intertwined; it is so clearly, so profoundly divine, that nobody could tell me there is something sinful here." Benz and Judy have a difficult time grappling with the beliefs of Fred and Jack. Benz is convinced their priorities are misguided, "It's really hard for me to wrap my head around right-wing Christians...on issues of poverty and class.... You can't crack open the New Testament and not run into that at least on every other page. I don't see how the religious Right has managed to make a political juggernaut out of everything else but that...That stuff has always been apparent to me." Although Judy is closely acquainted with Christians who support Bush and Cheney, this proximity has not resolved her questions, "I have people in my family who think Bush and Cheney are wonderful leaders. This is a challenge for me, to say the least. I love my family. I am called to love all God's children. I am pretty sure Jesus knows this is really hard sometimes."

A number of those interviewed contend that as their faith becomes more clear and more focused, uncertainty is less prevalent in their lives. Thus faith can be a lens that provides clarity and the stronger the faith, the more vivid, or intense, the clarity. Fred puts it this way, "The closer I get to God, the more black and white the issues become...those gray areas eventually go away." On the other side of the political spectrum, Benz has a similar sense of certainty, "I have a really hard time reading the Gospel without reading it as a mandate for social and economic equality...My politics is informed by my faith. And I've always had leftist politics as long as I've had politics, and they have always seemed to be absolutely self-apparent in the Gospel. No one had to tell me that. It just seemed right—completely, transparently, unavoidably true."

Like Benz, Fred's faith is, certainly, the most important influence in his life. He states simply, "My faith is who I am...It affects everything I do. It is who I am, I am a Christian." When he makes his political decisions, Fred filters his choices through three lenses: Christian first, conservative second, and Republican third "and a distant third." Herb agrees with Fred's hierarchy, everything except the party affiliation. Herb explains, "I give my loyalty to Christ before giving it to the Democratic Party. I understand that Christ's ways are radical, countercultural, and often not intuitive or even 'reasonable.' It is an alternate Way. I can't expect those outside the faith to ever fully live into those ideals, but I can work towards constantly nudging in that direction. In speaking to fellow Democrats I try not to lean in so far as to fall in."

It should not be surprising that the fervent beliefs of those who find themselves on opposite ends of the political spectrum are so similar in sentiment. Nor should it be unexpected that agonizingly painful divisions have arisen within the church as a result of the theological, and hence political, clarity of these faithful Christians.

For her part, Benz recognizes that some Christians wish she and others working within the church for the full inclusion of the gay community would focus on common efforts, like feeding the hungry or clothing the naked, and maybe let go of the gay agenda for awhile. She understands the request, but she cannot comply with it, "I get that from a pragmatic point—a pragmatic Christian desiring to do the work of God in the world. I just can't abide it as an answer, not only because I'm on the other side of the exclusive line on that particular issue, but because I don't think unity is a value that trumps all others." Acting upon her commitment to full inclusion is the only option for Benz if she is to remain faithful. Lisa shares Benz's reluctance to compromise. Lisa believes compromise, particularly on the issue of homosexuality, is untenable since the scripture should not be reinterpreted to suit the needs of a particular group. She explains, "The divisions come about when we're not willing to be obedient to the truth of scripture, when I want to adjust it to what fits me."

In spite of the formidable impasse that lies before them, as people of faith, these embattled Christians do find reasons to hope. They hope for a heart to be transformed. They hope that repentance will be forthcoming and forgiveness accepted. They hope that the true message of the Gospel will be revealed to a misguided flock.

Lisa has witnessed the power of God's Word to restore one who is lost, provided that person is willing to turn away from his or her sin, "So many groups have dug in their heels, homosexuals would just be one example, and said, 'This is who I am. This is my lifestyle so I am going to make my theology fit who I am and the rest of the church has to accept this with me.' From their perspective, if there's going to be unity, I have to make the move; and I'm not willing.... I don't think there is animosity towards the individual, but towards the sin, yes. I think the heterosexuals would be very open to that group coming back and saying, 'You're right. This is a bent that I have, just like some in this church are bent this way or that way, but I am going to do my best to live by the laws God has given.' In rare cases I have seen it happen." Fred agrees both that the Word can transform, and that Second Baptist would be ready to accept, the repentant sinner, "I don't feel our church is judgmental...If you've messed up, come on in.... We are all sinners, saved by grace...God's Word and the Holy Spirit will do the work."

Benz is equally convinced that transformation is possible, although she focuses less on God's Word and more on God's radical love to make it happen, "I persist in acting as though people change their minds. I'd go mad and sink into unbearable despair if I didn't. I think that people sometimes change their hearts and that helps them change their minds...Take the case of straight people warming up to the idea that homosexuality isn't a sin, or a "lifestyle"; that God made some of us queer, that God celebrates the diversity of human sexuality and we should, too. The most successful way to get people there is to put gay people in their path.... I believe that God acts on the human heart. Luckily, it is the human heart that is the site of God's most intense miracles. I don't need to judge whether other people are capable of being open to God's radical love and justice. I just act as though they are... I believe all people are redeemable."

For those who have found clarity along their religious journey, although reconciliation is theologically possible, this part of the path often seems elusive. But then there are those who find their lens of faith acts more like a prism, complicating one's vision in beautiful, yet perplexing ways and sometimes providing a glimpse of unexpected places. For this group, like the others, faith is the primary lens through which they view their lives, but what they see is not quite so distinct.

Obedience to his baptismal covenant guides every facet of Ben's life, "Our identity is developed out of our baptismal covenant and our obedience to it, which is first and foremost an obedience to love." And he rejects the notion that sexuality somehow trumps one's commitment as a follower of Jesus, "If you have claimed your baptism, your sexual orientation is secondary. I am not first a straight man; I am first a man that has chosen to follow Jesus. And that puts me into the church, not attraction to the opposite sex or to the same sex for that matter." At times he grows weary, frustrated by the amount of energy the institutional church spends focused on an issue that is barely mentioned in the Bible. Ben is troubled that who is included and who is excluded consumes so much of the church's resources. He sees a world in need and, "if somebody wants to help, fine, bring them in...The rest is a side issue."

Like the others, Tony's faith is central to all his decisions, especially his political decisions, "But not in a 'What Would Jesus Do?' type of thought process...If I have to ask myself that type of question in my daily decision-making process or when I vote, then I haven't the Christian faith I need to survive...I rely on His teachings and His being the center of my life to guide me in my ways." Tony is a faithful follower, but the path is not always clear. Tony admits that he did not know how he was going to vote in the 2004 presidential election until he entered the voting booth, and he now regrets having cast his vote for George W. Bush.

Ginny was raised in a theologically conservative household, but now finds herself pastoring a politically diverse congregation. She laments the increasing division within the church, "Polarization is the power of darkness. We can't dialogue with each other. I can't label myself; I don't know how someone else can label me." Ginny looks to the one she calls Lord and Savior to find some way out of the formidable impasse, "Jesus tells us there are those who 'have ears to hear' and there are some who simply will not hear. Perhaps some of us are called to be ear healers."

Ben also looks for a different way, "I don't necessarily think the Kingdom coming means that everyone will be a Christian, or at least I'm not sure that is the intention. Could it be that God has chosen to manifest Himself in different ways to different worldviews, or different cultures? That said, when John says that Jesus is the Way, the Truth, and the Life, I believe it. Jesus' way of witness is the only way that will save this world from self-destruction: turning the other cheek, praying for those who persecute us, feeding the hungry, eating with the sinner, and offering grace. Isn't evangelism about inviting people to join us in such a life?"

Perhaps it is precisely the imprecision that enables these Christians to see, however vague, some sort of common ground. For them the biblical mandate to feed the hungry, clothe the naked, and house the homeless is clear. Ginny puts it this way, "If we can just work alongside each other feeding the hungry, doing the things we can all agree that the Bible tells us to do, then the other stuff will follow."

Is one to conclude that those who claim a common ground are the peacemakers, the reconcilers, the heroes of this story and those who struggle to redeem the soul of their beloved church are somehow the story's villains?

Absolutely not. In fact, it's not that kind of story. The conflict within these tales will not be resolved. Though the purest forms of good and evil are woven through the narratives that fill these pages, in the end there is no victor; the triumph of these stories is in the telling.

Notes

CHAPTER 1

1. See, for example, Jim Wallis, *God's Politics* (San Francisco: HarperSanFrancisco, 2005); Andrew Kohut, John C. Green, Scott Keeter, and Robert C. Toth, *The Diminishing Divide: Religion's Changing Role in American Politics* (Washington, DC: Brookings Institution Press, 2000); and E.J. Dionne Jr., ed., *One Electorate Under God: A Dialogue on Religion and American Politics* (Washington, DC: Brookings Institution Press, 2004).

2. See, for example, Noah Feldman, *Divided by God: America's Church-State Problem—and What We Should Do About It* (New York: Farrar, Straus and Giroux, 2005).

3. Kohut et al., *The Diminishing Divide*, 1.

4. Alan Cooperman, "Religious Right, Left Meet in the Middle: Clergy Aim to Show That Faith Unifies," *Washington Post*, June 15, 2005.

5. See, for example, recent studies on voting patterns in Michigan. John C. Green and Mark Silk, "Why Moral Values Did Count," *Religion in the News*, Spring 2005.

6. John Danforth, *Faith and Politics: How the "Moral Values" Debate Divides America and How to Move Forward Together* (New York: Viking, 2006).

7. Rick Warren, *The Purpose-Driven Life* (Philadelphia: Miniature Editions, 2003).

8. The preceding information came from InfoServ, the information service of The United Methodist Church. 2006 United Methodist Communications.

9. Presidents@presidentusa.net copyright 2002 by CB Presidential Research Services.

10. Ibid.

11. Presbyterian Church (USA).

12. The Baptist Faith and Message: Article 1.

13. Southern Baptist Convention Copyright 1999–2006.

14. Presidents@presidentusa.net.

CHAPTER 2

Interviews were conducted in Charlotte, North Carolina, February 24–26, 2006.

1. The Disciple Bible Studies are a series of study programs produced by The United Methodist Church that stress the connection between biblical knowledge and Christian leadership.

2. John Edward is a medium, lecturer, and author whose books include *One Last Time: A Psychic Medium Speaks to Those We Have Loved and Lost* (New York: Berkley Publishing Group, 1999).

3. A district superintendent is an ordained minister appointed by a bishop to supervise the pastors and local churches in a district.

4. Dorothy Day, *The Long Loneliness* (New York: Harper & Row, 1952).

5. Karen Armstrong, scholar and former Roman Catholic nun, is the author of, among others, *A History of God: The 4,000-Year Quest of Judaism, Christianity and Islam* (New York: Alfred A. Knopf, 1994).

6. The AMEZ denomination was founded in the early 1800s after African-American members were forced out of John Street Methodist Chapel in New York City. In the past decade the UMC and the AMEZ have been working toward denominational cooperation and possible merger.

7. *The Upper Room* is a bimonthly daily devotional guide with short meditations written by Christians around the world and published by The United Methodist Church.

CHAPTER 3

Interviews were conducted in Delaware, Ohio, November 11–13, 2005.

1. In the Presbyterian tradition, a local congregation "calls" or hires its clergy out of an approved pool of applicants. In The United Methodist Church, clergy are appointed to congregations by a bishop.

2. There are currently 14 Catholic churches in Charleston and 30 Catholic churches in the state. New Advent Catholic Encyclopedia.

3. Young Life is a national and international ministry focused on engaging teenagers in positive "mentor" relationships and converting them to Christianity.

CHAPTER 4

Interviews were conducted in Houston, Texas, October 6–9, 2006.

1. Kellye Williams, *Exodus 32—God's People Disobey,* Second Baptist Church Third-Grade Class Skit, October 7, 2006.

2. Ibid.

3. Ibid.

4. Ibid.

5. The Great Commission is a component of Christianity focusing on mission work and evangelism originating from the instruction of Jesus that his followers must go out into the world and teach and baptize others.

6. Second Baptist Church is one church with six locations throughout Houston: the Woodway Campus, which is the focus of this chapter, the West Campus, the North Campus, the Pearland Campus, the Willowbrook Campus, and the Cypress Campus.

7. The Family Research Council is a conservative, Christian, nonprofit think tank and lobbying group founded by James Dobson in 1981. Tony Perkins is currently the group's president.

8. The Campaign for Working Families is a nonpartisan political action committee, founded by Gary Bauer in 1996, focused on supporting profamily, pro-life, and pro–free enterprise candidates in their bids for elected office on the state and national levels.

9. Bible Study Fellowship (BSF) is an international, interdenominational group that offers Bible study opportunities for children, men, and women in 35 countries.

10. See, for example, Dr. Ed Young, *Culture Wars: The Battle for the Next Generation* (Houston: Winning Walk Family, 2004).

11. Ibid., 7–14.

12. Dr. Ed Young, *The Promise of Peace and Deliverance* (Houston: Winning Walk Ministries, October 8, 2006).

13. Ibid.

14. Ibid.

15. Christian Smith with Melinda Lundquist Denton, *Soul Searching: The Religious and Spiritual Lives of American Teenagers* (New York: Oxford University Press, 2005).

16. See, for example, 1 Timothy 3:2.

CHAPTER 5

Interviews were conducted in Brooklyn, New York, over a number of months. The first was September 7, 2005, and the last was November 28, 2005.

1. The Judicial Council is the denomination's highest judicial body.

2. The Reconciling Movement within The United Methodist Church (UMC) was founded in 1982 in response to antigay legislation passed by the UMC. The Reconciling Movement seeks the full participation of gay and lesbian people at all levels of the church.

3. The New York Annual Conference of the UMC is one of 63 regional bodies within the United States and includes southern New York and western Connecticut.

4. General Conference is the highest legislative body in The United Methodist Church. The voting membership consists of an equal number of clergy and lay delegates elected by the annual conferences. General Conference convenes every four years. It is the only body that can speak officially for the denomination.

5. *The Book of Discipline of the United Methodist Church 2004* (Nashville, TN: Abingdon Press, 2005).

6. The *lectio divina* is a form of meditation first used by the Benedictine monks. It involves a slow, thoughtful praying of the Word of God and an emphasis on silence in order that one might be able to hear the still, small voice of God.

7. The United Methodist Church has an itinerant system in which ordained ministers are sent by a bishop to a field of service. District superintendents oversee several dozen congregations and assist the bishop in assigning clergy to appointments.

8. K. Killian Noe, *Finding Our Way Home: Addictions and Divine Love* (Scottdale, PA: Herald Press, 2003).

9. "What is a labyrinth? It is a path of prayer, a walking meditation that can become a mirror of the soul. . . . The path becomes a metaphor for our own spiritual journey. A labyrinth is not a maze. A maze is designed for you to lose your way; a labyrinth is designed for you to find your way." [Foreword by Rev. Dr. Lauren Artress in Jill Kimberly Hartwell Geoffrion, *Praying the Labyrinth* (Cleveland, OH: The Pilgrim Press, 1999), vii.]

10. During these classes participants from the same district of The United Methodist Church join together to develop lay-ministry skills.

11. Daniel A. Helminiak, *What the Bible Really Says about Homosexuality* (San Francisco: Alamo Square Press, 1994); Sue Monk Kidd, *The Secret Life of Bees* (New York: Viking, 2002); Philip Yancey, *Soul Survivor: How My Faith Survived the Church* (New York: Doubleday, 2001).

12. The lectionary is a sequence of Bible passages used in church services throughout the year. It includes passages from the Old Testament and the New Testament to be read in a three-year cycle.

13. Compiled by Carmen Acevedo Butcher, *Incandescence: 365 Readings with Women Mystics* (Brewster, MA: Paraclete Press, 2005).

14. Walter J. Harrelson, ed., *The New Interpreter's Study Bible* (Nashville: Abingdon Press, 2003).

15. Donald Miller, *Blue Like Jazz: Nonreligious Thoughts on Christian Spirituality* (Nashville: Nelson, 2003), 47.

16. Geoffrion, *Praying the Labyrinth,* 22.

CHAPTER 6

1. Laurie Goodstein, "Religious Voting Data Show Some Shift, Observers Say," *New York Times,* November 9, 2006.

2. Diana Butler Bass, "Not Red, Not Blue. . .Purple Churches," in God's Politics," a blog by Jim Wallis [electronic bulletin board], November 2, 2006, http://www.beliefnet.com/blogs/godspolitics (accessed November 3, 2006).

3. Ibid.

4. Ibid.

Index

About the Author

CHARLENE FLOYD teaches religion and politics in the Doctor of Ministry Program at New York Theological Seminary. A political scientist, she has been studying religion and politics for over twenty years.